in

ENGINEERING

GERALDINE GARNER

SECOND EDITION

VGM Career Books

Chicago New York San Francisco Lisbon London Madrid Mexico City
Milan New Delhi San Juan Seoul Singapore Sydney Toronto

Library of Congress Cataloging-in-Publication Data

Garner, Geraldine O.
  Careers in engineering / Geraldine Garner.—2nd ed.
      p.   cm—(VGM professional careers series)
    ISBN 0-07-139041-3 (paperback)
    1. Engineering—Vocational guidance.   I. Title.   II. Series.

  TA157.G3267   2002
  620'.0023'73—dc21   2002027208

3 4 5 6 7 8 9 0   DOC/DOC   0 9 8 7 6 5

ISBN 0-07-139041-3

McGraw-Hill books are available at special quantity discounts to use as premiums and sales promotions, or for use in corporate training programs. For more information, please write to the Director of Special Sales, Professional Publishing, McGraw-Hill, Two Penn Plaza, New York, NY 10121-2298. Or contact your local bookstore.

This book is printed on acid-free paper.

This book is dedicated to Lauren, John, Adrian, Richelle, and Avery.

CONTENTS

CHAPTER 20
Engineering Technology   185
Technology Specialists • Education and Other Qualifications •
Outlook for the Future • Earnings • Additional Sources of
Information

APPENDIX A
U.S. Universities Offering Engineering Programs   197

APPENDIX B
Scholarships   209

APPENDIX C
General Engineering Societies   217

APPENDIX D
ABET Member Societies and Disciplines   221

Engineering: A Career That Makes Our Society Better

CHAPTER

WHAT IS ENGINEERING?

Engineering has often been compared to both art and science. According to Henry Petroski, in *To Engineer Is Human*, "Engineering does share traits with both art and science, for engineering is a human endeavor that is both creative and analytical." However, engineering is not science or art.

Scientists discover and explain physical nature. Engineers create solutions to human problems using the principles discovered by scientists and mathematicians. It is often said that engineers are an extremely creative group of people! They are problem-solvers. They invent new things that we need, and they improve things that are not working well for us.

Just look around you and you will see the creativity and beauty of engineers' work. From the Golden Gate Bridge in San Francisco to the space shuttle to a high-tech operating room in today's hospitals, you see the work of engineers. Consider just some of the engineering marvels that touch our daily lives: digital televisions, boom boxes, personal computers, cell phones, microwave ovens, snowblowers, jet skis, race cars, thermal coats, disposable cameras, compact hair dryers, frozen pizzas, the Internet! The list can go on and on.

What is an engineer? Many definitions have been written. The American Society of Engineering Education says, "Engineering is the profession in which a knowledge of the mathematical and natural sciences gained by study, experience, and practice is applied with judgment to develop ways to utilize the materials and forces of nature, economically for the benefit of mankind."

A more concise definition appears on "Discover Engineering Online," discoverengineering.org/eweek/about_eng.htm: "Engineering is the application of math and science to create something of value from our natural resources."

No matter which definition appeals to you, there is no mistake. Engineers are creative problem-solvers who rely on the discoveries of math and science to improve the world in which we live. That is why Raymond Landis, dean of engineering and technology at California State University in Los Angeles, in his book *Studying Engineering*, lists ten rewards of an engineering career:

1. Job satisfaction
2. Variety of career opportunities
3. Challenging work
4. Intellectual development
5. Potential to benefit society
6. Financial security
7. Prestige
8. Professional environment
9. Technological and scientific discovery
10. Creative thinking

A HISTORY OF ENGINEERING

Having stated that engineers are creative problem-solvers, one could come to the conclusion that engineering is a new career field that has emerged as a result of the many inventions of the twentieth century that dramatically changed the way people live. While it is true that the field of engineering has changed and grown in recent years, engineering is a very established career field with a long and distinguished history.

The first engineer known by name and achievement is Imhotep, who built the famous stepped pyramid in Egypt circa 2550 B.C. The Persians, Greeks, and Romans, along with the Egyptian civilization, took engineering to remarkable heights by using arithmetic, geometry, and physical science. Many famous ancient structures that are still standing today demonstrate the ingenuity and skill of these early pioneers of engineering.

Medieval European engineers, like the ancient engineers, combined military and civil skills to carry construction to heights unknown by the ancients. They developed techniques known as the Gothic arch and flying buttress. The sketchbook of Villard de Honnecourt, who lived and worked in the early thirteenth century, demonstrates the Gothic engineer's remarkable knowledge of natural and physical science, mathematics, geometry, and draftsmanship.

In Japan, China, India, and other Far Eastern areas, engineering developed separately but similarly. Sophisticated techniques of construction, hydraulics, and metallurgy practiced in the Far East led to the impressive, beautiful cities of the Mongol Empire.

In 1747, the first use of the term *civil engineer* coincided with the founding in France of the first engineering school, the National School of Bridges and Highways. Its graduates researched and formalized theories on many subjects, including fluid pressure. John Smeaton (1724–1792), British designer of the Eddystone Lighthouse, was the first to actually call himself a civil engineer, thus separating his work from that of the military engineer. The eighteenth century also witnessed the founding in Britain of the world's first engineering society, the Institution of Civil Engineers.

Civil engineers of the nineteenth century designed sanitation and water-supply systems, laid out highways and railroads, and planned cities. Mechanical engineering had its beginnings in England and Scotland and came out of the inventions of Scottish engineer James Watt and the textile machinists of the Industrial Revolution. The rise of the British machine-tool industry caused interest in the study of mechanical engineering to skyrocket, both in Europe and abroad.

The gradual growth of knowledge in the area of electricity in the nineteenth century eventually led to the most popular branch of the engineering profession of today—electrical and electronics engineering. Electronics engineering came into prominence through the work of various English and German scientists in the nineteenth century and with the development in the United States of the vacuum tube and the transistor in the twentieth century. Electrical and electronics engineers now outnumber all other engineers in the world.

Chemical engineering has come into existence through the nineteenth-century spread of industrial processes involving chemical reactions to produce textiles, food, metals, and a variety of other materials. By 1880, the use of chemicals in manufacturing had created a new industry, mass production of chemicals. The design and operation of this industry's plants became the main function of the new chemical engineer.

The twentieth century brought many other branches of the profession into prominence, and the number of people working in the engineering field has increased dramatically. Artificial hearts, airplanes, computers, lasers, plastics, space travel, nuclear energy, and television are only a few of the scientific and technological breakthroughs that engineers helped to bring about from 1900 to 2000. There is no doubt the field will continue to grow and expand in the twenty-first century.

MAJOR ENGINEERING AREAS AND SPECIALTIES

Although the U.S. Department of Labor lists twenty-five engineering specialties with at least eighty-five different subdivisions, it is important to keep in mind that there are six areas of engineering that form the core of the profession. These areas are:

- Chemical engineering
- Civil engineering
- Electrical engineering
- Industrial engineering
- Materials science engineering
- Mechanical engineering

Preparation in any one of these areas will provide a solid foundation for a wide range of specialties.

Undergraduate study in any one of these areas will be adequate preparation for many career options after graduation, including graduate study in the same area or another area of engineering. Study of one of these basic areas of engineering is also excellent preparation for the study of business, law, or medicine. In a time when it is important to keep many options open for future career development, pursuit of one of these disciplines can provide flexibility and satisfaction throughout one's professional life.

Over the years each traditional branch of engineering has developed increasingly more focused specialties. Today some of those specialties have become engineering professions in their own right.

There are other engineering areas that can either be pursued as a specialty area within one of the previously discussed engineering disciplines or pursued as a college major in their own right at institutions that offer a more in-depth preparation for these fields. Some of these fields include:

- Aerospace engineering
- Agricultural engineering
- Automotive engineering
- Biomedical engineering
- Computer engineering
- Environmental engineering
- Manufacturing engineering
- Petroleum engineering

This group of engineering areas allows one to specialize in an industry or a particular application of engineering knowledge. These fields are discussed further in this book.

THE TECHNOLOGY TEAM

It is evident that engineers address the challenges that face the society in which they live. From the Egyptian pyramids and the compounds for medieval swords to composite tennis rackets, engineers are problem-solvers. They link scientific discovery with day-to-day applications.

Engineers are team players who improve products, processes, and services. Therefore, it is important to understand the technology team on which engineers participate.

The engineer is a part of a team of specialists whose goal is to apply scientific knowledge and practical experience to the solution of problems. This "technology team" is a workforce consisting of scientists, engineers, technicians, and craftsworkers. Everyone on the team works together to solve a problem or to invent a useful device or system. In learning about the makeup and function of the technology team, you can develop an understanding of technology as a whole and of how it is put to use.

At one end of the spectrum of technology is the scientist. The scientist's purpose is to discover knowledge. He or she seeks to uncover new facts and to learn more truths about the natural world. Furthermore, scientists seek to explain the facts that they discover by developing new theorems or theories that relate causes and effects in the natural systems they have investigated. In their work, scientists seek to know rather than to apply. In other words, their principal concern is not the application of the new knowledge they have discovered but simply the discovery of that knowledge itself. Some scientists are interested in developing applications of science and scientific methods, but the principal activity of even these individuals remains the discovery of new knowledge.

In contrast to the scientist, the engineer is interested primarily in the application of scientific knowledge about the natural world and in discovering facts about the artificial world created by humans. The primary responsibility of engineers, as a part of the technology team, is in conceiving and planning efforts to apply scientific knowledge. They design and plan developmental projects, production processes, operations and maintenance procedures, and so on. Their activities are devoted to designs and plans to achieve certain results. These results almost always benefit society; however, the purpose beyond that is to achieve this benefit at a minimum cost in money, materials, and time. In an effort to achieve efficient results, the engineers attempt to forecast the behavior of a system they have designed or to predict the accomplishments of a planned program. All the benefits and costs of proposed activities must be predicted by engineers, who are the principal planners of the technology team.

It is the technician's responsibility to see that the engineer's design or plan is implemented. While the engineer is concerned mainly with designing or conceiving, the technician is concerned with doing. The technician may be involved in time-and-motion studies or in supervising the construction of a facility designed and planned by the engineer. In accomplishing such work, the engineering technician is more specialized and more concerned with a particular application of scientific knowledge than is the engineer who must plan complex systems. Basically, the technician utilizes science and mathematics to solve technical problems contained within the broad framework of designs and plans conceived by an engineer. Additionally, he or she utilizes instruments and certain tools to measure and monitor the quality and performance of completed systems. However, the technician's principal function is not to utilize tools but to see that designs and plans are implemented by the craftsworkers who do use tools. The technician lies in the occupational spectrum closest to the engineer.

At the opposite end of the technology spectrum from the scientist are the skilled craftsworkers, who use their hands and special skills rather than science or scientific knowledge. They are more likely to employ tools than instruments in their work, and they must develop a high degree of skill in using these tools. Craftsworkers include electricians, instrument makers, machinists, model makers, and others. The craftsworker, too, has an important position on the technology team, and, to some degree, the overall success of the technical system depends upon his or her skill in utilizing tools and his or her concern for good workmanship in construction.

WHAT AN ENGINEER DOES

Engineers plan, design, construct, and manage the use of natural and human resources. In addition to human skill, engineering also involves science, mathematics, and aesthetics. As stated before, engineers solve problems. They design cars, spacecraft, and medical devices; they can build buildings and bridges; they solve environmental problems; they apply computer technology to a wide range of problems. Because engineers have a strong interest and ability in science, mathematics, and technology, they are team leaders who can take an idea from concept to reality.

There are seven major functions common to all branches of engineering.

- *Research.* A research engineer looks for new principles and processes by using scientific and mathematical concepts, by experimenting, or by using inductive reasoning.
- *Development.* A development engineer takes the results of the research and puts it to use. Creative and intelligent application of new ideas may give the world a working model of a new machine, chemical process, or computer chip.

- *Design.* A design engineer chooses the methods and materials necessary to meet technical requirements and performance specifications when a new product is being designed.
- *Construction.* A construction engineer prepares the construction site, arranges the materials, and organizes personnel and equipment.
- *Production.* A production engineer takes care of plant layout and the choosing of equipment with regard to the human and economic factors. He or she selects processes and tools, checks the flow of materials and components, and does testing and inspection.
- *Operation.* An operating engineer controls manufacturing and processing plants and machines. He or she determines procedures and supervises the workforce.
- *Management.* Engineers in the management area analyze customer needs, solve economic problems, and deal in a variety of other areas depending on the type of organization involved.

Even within the different branches of engineering, there is no one generic engineer. There exists a wide variety of areas in which the prospective engineer can find satisfying and rewarding work.

In addition to diversity of function, engineering is also performed in a wide variety of private, commercial, and government settings. Many engineers are found in manufacturing industries, but they are also found in nonmanufacturing settings such as banks and hospitals. In addition, they work in engineering and architectural firms; public utilities; business and management consulting firms; federal, state, and local governments; and colleges and universities.

CAREER PATH SCENARIOS

According to *Great Jobs for Engineering Majors*, there are five primary career paths that engineers follow: the industry, consulting, government, academic, and Internet career paths.

The Industry Career Path

The first career path is in industry. According to Garner, "Industry has always provided engineers with an abundant and diverse range of career paths leading to personal and professional growth." However, the industry career path has undergone dramatic changes in recent years, and the old image of industry is no longer accurate. Most industrial settings are now high-tech workplaces demanding high levels of engineering expertise to solve problems related to researching, developing, and designing new products and then to manufacturing those products in a cost-efficient manner. Some of the other areas of industry in which engineers tend to work are accounting and finance, administration, information systems processing, marketing and sales, and technical/professional services.

Therefore, there are numerous opportunities for leadership responsibilities in the industrial setting, and these opportunities are coming earlier and earlier in engineers' careers because of the demand for the new knowledge that graduating engineers possess. The industrial career path can lead engineers to the executive level in many companies. That is because engineers understand product design, manufacture, and distribution. In addition, it is most likely that engineers in industry will have obtained advanced degrees in business administration during the course of their employment. This means that they not only have knowledge of the engineering side of the industry but also of the business side. Therefore, they can become strong candidates for positions such as plant manager, vice president, president, and even chief executive officer (CEO).

The Consulting Career Path

The second career path is in consulting. In this career path, engineers work for companies that are hired by other companies to perform engineering tasks, design tasks, or management tasks. What exactly does this mean?

Engineers who work for engineering consulting firms perform engineering tasks for other companies or organizations, and when their job is done they move on to a new project with another company or organization. For example, if your city or town wanted to build a new highway for the new mall that is being constructed, officials would be most likely to hire a company that has many civil engineers who are knowledgeable about how to design and build highways and bridges in a cost-effective manner. That engineering consulting company would come to the city and build the new highway, and when the engineers were finished they would go on to work on another highway project for another neighborhood, city, or state that needed their expertise.

Engineers who work for design consulting firms do the work necessary to design a device for another company that wants to offer a new product to its customers. For example, if a company wanted to make new in-line skates that are lighter and faster, it could hire a design consulting firm that has engineers who would work only on the new skate design until it met the requirements of the company that had hired them. Once the company could use the design to manufacture new in-line skates in a cost-effective manner, the design consulting firm would begin working on another product for another company.

All consulting engineers work on numerous projects with different types of organizations and people. Some engineers pursue consulting careers early to help them decide where they ultimately want to work, and others pursue consulting later in their careers when they have become real experts in their field—at this point clients are willing to pay them very well for their knowledge.

The Government Career Path

A third career path for engineers is in government. Federal, state, and local governments are excellent employers. For example, NASA employs many types of engineers in the space program. While many aerospace engineers are employed by this government agency, NASA facilities also hire almost every type of engineer because of the great diversity and creativity of its projects. Likewise, organizations like the FBI, CIA, and National Security Agency hire all types of engineers, and particularly those with strong foreign language abilities.

While the U.S. Environmental Protection Agency and the U.S. Army Corps of Engineers employ many civil and environmental engineers, there are also numerous career paths for these engineers in state departments of transportation and environmental protection agencies throughout the country. According to *Great Jobs for Engineering Majors*, "The Food and Drug Administration is a major employer of biomedical engineers, while the U.S. Department of Defense continues to employ a wide variety of engineers in both civilian and enlisted positions for its agencies and installations throughout the world."

The Academic Career Path

The fourth career path for engineers is the academic path. This means that many engineers teach. While most engineers who teach have received either master's or Ph.D. degrees and teach in colleges and universities, some engineers decide to obtain state teaching certificates after completing their bachelor's degree. The teaching certificate qualifies them to teach math and/or science in middle schools and high schools in the state in which they live.

Engineers who pursue the academic career path enjoy the process of sharing knowledge with others. They may have had experience teaching or tutoring and know that this is satisfying to them. In most cases, engineers who teach in middle schools and high schools, as well as those who teach in colleges and universities, have looked at their personal values, strengths, and interests and determined that teaching is the best career path for them.

The Internet Career Path

Finally, a new career path for engineers emerged in the 1990s. The Internet career path has opened new possibilities for graduating engineers. The phenomenon of the Internet was developed by engineers and continues to provide many career opportunities for them, whether they are electrical and computer engineers or industrial engineers and computer scientists.

While there are Internet opportunities for engineers with companies that are closely associated with the Internet, like Amazon.com, Ebay, or Priceline.com, there are also Internet career possibilities with more traditional companies such as GE, General Motors, or Delta Airlines. These companies have realized that to be successful now they need to use the Internet to get their products to their customers more quickly and more cost effectively.

Despite the crash of tech stocks at the beginning of the twenty-first century, this is a technology and a lifestyle that is not going to disappear. Therefore, increasing numbers of career path opportunities will exist for engineers who possess the right set of skills in the future.

Other Career Paths for Engineers

In addition to these engineering career paths, many engineering graduates decide to pursue graduate and professional degrees. While some obtain advanced degrees in engineering, others decide to pursue graduate and professional degrees in such areas as medicine and law. These advanced degrees offer increased opportunities for career advancement in any career path the individual pursues.

FUTURE PROJECTIONS

Many factors in today's global economy suggest that the future projections for engineering are excellent. This is especially true in areas such as electrical and computer engineering, environmental engineering, materials engineering, manufacturing engineering, and biomedical engineering.

However, engineering opportunities have always had a tendency to go in cycles. Aerospace engineering is a good example, as is chemical engineering. The changing economy and world events impact opportunities for engineering. For example, military actions in the world require innovations in surveillance equipment and defense technologies. Likewise, new discoveries about DNA lead to innovations in pharmaceuticals. This means that new and emerging industries will allow competition in a global market. The electronics and health-care industries are examples of growing industries that are providing new opportunities for engineers.

Federal and state governments regularly publish documents that provide current and up-to-date information on the future outlook and projections that apply to a wide range of career fields. The *Occupational Outlook Handbook* (bls.gov/ocol) published by the U.S. Department of Labor is a good source of information in this area. But a word to the wise—in deciding which engineering area you wish to pursue, do not rely solely on information about the engineering disciplines that are currently in demand. There are always openings for all types of engineers. Therefore, it is best to pursue the area that relies on your personal strengths and is of most interest to *you*!

Studying what interests you will most likely be easier and, therefore, you are more likely to do better in your course work. Good grades in any engineering major will assure that job opportunities and graduate school study are future options. However, the most important reason for pursuing what most interests you is that you will be more likely to be successful and satisfied with your career choice in the future.

CHAPTER 2

PREPARING FOR A SUCCESSFUL ENGINEERING CAREER

Unlike many other career fields, preparation for an engineering career begins early. The math and science that you take in middle school begin to open doors for you to study engineering in college. However, if you do not take the recommended math and science in middle school and high school, do not give up your dream of becoming an engineer. Look into community college courses in math and science or consider summer school courses at your school to get caught up. The field of engineering needs more well-prepared people. Take the time, make the effort, and prepare to join this profession that makes our way of life and quality of life what it is today and what it can be in the future.

WHAT SHOULD YOU DO BEFORE GOING TO COLLEGE?

Prior to entering a college or university to study engineering, it is very important to take as many mathematics classes at the high school level as possible. These courses should be algebra I and II, geometry, trigonometry, and calculus. In addition, it is important to take as many science courses as possible. These courses should include biology, chemistry, and physics. Chemistry and physics are required courses in undergraduate engineering programs; therefore, you should take as many chemistry and physics courses as possible at your high school, particularly honors and advanced placement courses. English, social studies, and foreign language courses are all necessary for admission to college engineering programs. Computer and economics courses are also recommended.

To be sure that you meet the basic educational requirements that will be expected when you enter an engineering major in college, it is important to compare the courses you will have taken to those that the National Society of Professional Engineers recommends:

Algebra I and II
Geometry
Trigonometry
Calculus
Biology
Chemistry
Physics
English (four units)
Social studies (three units)
Foreign languages (two to three units)
Fine arts/humanities (one or two units)
Computer programming or computer applications

Other courses that may be helpful include history and public speaking. It is also recommended that prospective engineering students take advanced placement (AP) or honors-level courses, particularly in math and science. It is advisable to set a goal of achieving combined scores of at least 1000 on the SAT exam or 20 on the ACT exam.

Today most admissions officers at engineering colleges and universities are also looking for well-rounded students. Extracurricular activities during high school are important in reflecting this. Being a member of math- and science-related clubs will demonstrate strong and consistent interests related to engineering. However, participation in athletics, student government, service organizations, and cultural activities are also important. All of these activities demonstrate ability to work with other people and to lead groups.

In addition to the information in this book, it is recommended that you obtain more information about careers in engineering from counselors and teachers. You can also obtain information from the local chapter of the

National Society of Professional Engineers or the local chapters of professional associations in the field of engineering in which you have an interest. The Junior Engineering Technical Society (JETS) exists for the purpose of furnishing information to high school students interested in careers in engineering, technology, science, and mathematics. One of its primary activities is the sponsorship of JETS chapters in junior highs and high schools. These chapters, in turn, sponsor extracurricular clubs, under the supervision of a faculty advisor assisted by a volunteer professional engineer from the community. The typical JETS chapter or club holds regular meetings at which members explore various aspects of the field of engineering, technology, science, and mathematics. The club may visit local industries, consulting firms, and government agencies to discuss their interests with practicing engineers and scientists. Programs, projects, and other group activities are part of most clubs' programs.

Information concerning JETS can be obtained from any local chapter or from the JETS, 1420 King Street, Suite 405, Alexandria, VA 22314 (jets.org).

HOW TO CHOOSE A COLLEGE

The next step in pursuing an engineering career is the selection of a college or university where you will study the engineering field of your choice. College and university websites and catalogs are important tools in comparing and evaluating engineering education programs. Appendix A provides a listing of all U.S. colleges and universities that offer engineering degrees. It is important to learn how to read these institutions' Web pages and catalogs so that you will be able to ask good questions and get full information on the requirements and expectations of each program.

The first step is to look at entrance requirements. Many colleges and universities have minimum entrance requirements. If you are not sure if you meet the entrance requirements, you should speak to the admissions officers of the colleges or universities in which you are interested. Admissions officers will be willing to discuss how they evaluate applications.

The second step is to look at the engineering majors and specialties that are offered at each college or university. Do the colleges and universities that you are considering offer the type of engineering major in which you are interested? Will you have to maintain a certain grade point average in order to declare a major in your area of interest? If a certain grade point average is required to declare a major, what percentage of entering students are able to maintain the average required for the major in which you are interested? If you are unsure about your major, does the school provide a broad enough introduction to engineering that you will have sufficient options and time in order to select a major? Does the school provide a support system to help you decide on a major, or are you expected to reach this decision on your own?

The college catalog should tell you the cost of tuition, fees, and room and board. However, it is important to keep in mind that these will not be your only costs. You will buy books, travel to and from school, buy personal supplies, pay for entertainment expenses, and incur other day-to-day costs. Therefore, it will be important to look at the availability of financial aid. Be sure to ask each college or university that you are considering to provide you with information on all grants, scholarships, loans, ROTC, and work-study programs that may help you finance your education. However, it is always advisable to meet with the financial aid director to discuss your specific needs.

"College Nights" are an excellent opportunity to gather information on admissions requirements, costs of attendance, and financial aid opportunities. Start going to these events throughout your high school experience, and get to know the admissions people. However, nothing substitutes for a visit to the college campus. It is important to see and feel the campus environment as well as the engineering environment. That is the best way to determine if there will be a good fit between you and the college you choose to attend.

HOW TO MANAGE YOUR ENGINEERING CAREER WHILE IN COLLEGE

Your career in engineering will not start when you leave college. It will actually start while you are an undergraduate student. When you pick a major (mechanical engineering, chemical engineering, biomedical engineering, etc.) you have taken the first step in your career. It is not an irreversible step, but it is a step!

Bachelor's-degree programs in engineering are available at colleges or universities accredited by the Accreditation Board of Engineering and Technology (ABET). These programs take four or five years.

In general, the first two years concentrate on mathematics and the physical sciences, with introductory engineering courses and courses in English and the social sciences. The last two years include required courses in engineering and particularly required courses in the major. In addition, engineering students take technical electives and "free" electives. Free electives are either any course outside of engineering that the student wishes to take or any course on a list of electives approved by the engineering department. Technical electives are usually engineering courses from disciplines outside of one's major.

There are also transfer programs called "two-plus-two" or "two-plus-three" programs. These programs combine two years of study at a community college and then two or three more years of study after transferring to a participating four-year college. In some cases, both bachelor's and master's degrees are awarded at the end of a "two-plus-three" program.

There are also five- or six-year cooperative engineering education programs. In these programs, engineering students alternate periods of academic study with periods of paid engineering-related work in industry.

Most bachelor's-degree programs in engineering are available through colleges or universities that are accredited by the Accreditation Board of Engineering and Technology (ABET). To become an accredited engineering or engineering technology program by ABET, each engineering department must demonstrate that its program has published educational objectives and that it is continually assessing and evaluating how those objectives are being achieved by its graduates. In addition, ABET requires that each engineering student be able to demonstrate a specific set of minimum outcomes at the time of graduation.

In order for an academic program to achieve these student outcomes, the faculty must look not only at curriculum but at the total experience that students have, including the skill sets they bring from high school as well as the co-op and extracurricular experience they have in college. When looking at engineering schools and specific engineering programs, it is important to consider the educational objectives that they have set for their program and the resources they provide to help students achieve the required outcomes. Careful examination of the school's and the program's website is very important.

To locate accredited engineering programs, begin by going to ABET's website, abet.org/accredited_prgs.html. In addition to looking at college and university websites, it is recommended that students become familiar with the criteria that selected professional associations have set for their chosen discipline. ABET is made up of member societies that can help you not only understand careers in their specific field of engineering, but also their recommended criteria for engineering education in that field. In addition, many of these societies offer scholarships to deserving individuals. See Appendix B for scholarship information and Appendix D for ABET member societies.

In an accredited engineering program students are required to spend the first two years studying basic sciences: mathematics, physics, chemistry, and introductory engineering. They also take humanities, social sciences, and English. During the last two years, most courses are in engineering. It is during this time that students can elect to specialize in one area within their discipline or complete a general engineering degree in their chosen area of engineering.

The engineering experience that you gain during your college career should extend beyond your classes and labs. Internships and summer jobs in an engineering setting can be important to your career. However, many engineering employers place more value on cooperative engineering education experience.

Co-op is an engineering educational approach that began at the University of Cincinnati in 1906 when Professor Herman Schneider's research indicated that it was too costly for engineering employers to train new engineers after graduation. For nearly one hundred years, hundreds of thousands of engineers have alternated periods of paid work experience related to their major with periods of academic course work. These co-op graduates completed their undergraduate education with a four-year degree and more than one year of increasingly responsible engineering experience. Many collegiate engineering schools offer cooperative education programs. Generally these are five-year programs, and numerous studies have indicated that the fifth year is well worth the investment. Year after year sur-veys have shown that the starting salaries of co-op engineering graduates have been significantly higher than those of non co-op graduates. How-ever, most co-op graduates will say that the real benefit of the program is the experience they gained and the increased awareness of what they enjoy and want to do as professional engineers.

While there are many outstanding co-op programs, those at the Uni-versity of Cincinnati, the University of Detroit, Drexel University, North-western University, Purdue University, Georgia Institute of Technology, Northeastern University, and Virginia Polytechnic Institute and State Uni-versity (Virginia Tech) are among the oldest engineering co-op programs in the country.

BEYOND THE UNDERGRADUATE DEGREE—WORK OR GRADUATE SCHOOL

When the bachelor's degree in engineering is awarded, the recipients have many options open to them. If you receive a B.S. degree in engineering you can choose to pursue your engineering career in a wide variety of areas such as industry, business, consulting, marketing, management, government, research, university teaching, sales, and the military.

In addition to the numerous employment options that engineers have, many engineers eventually pursue study beyond the bachelor's degree. Some go on to medical school or law school. Others obtain graduate degrees in business or management. However, many pursue master's and doctoral degrees in engineering disciplines.

PROFESSIONAL LICENSING

After graduation from college, engineering is a field in which you can become a registered or licensed engineer in the state or states in which you work. Engineers who become registered or licensed are known as "profes-sional engineers." They are able to put the designation P.E. after their names. This designation conveys a level of commitment to the engineering profession that is highly valued in a number of industries and engineering disciplines.

According to the National Council of Examiners for Engineering (NCEE), there is a growing demand for engineers who have become licensed engineers. In part, this demand is due to the perception that P.E.s are committed to the highest ethical and work standards and to their own futures and the future of the profession.

Many employers want P.E.s on their team because the designation of P.E. provides credibility to clients and to customers. In very competitive fields within engineering this can be an important advantage. For civil engineers and for engineers with consulting engineering firms the designation of P.E. is not just an advantage, it is often a requirement. In some industries the P.E. designation is highly recommended for management positions. Consequently, becoming a licensed engineer could be one of the most important career decisions you will make.

The NCEE identifies the following benefits of becoming a P.E.:

- *Promotability.* Many employers require licensure for advancement to senior engineering positions. This is particularly true when companies are engaged in internal and external partnership agreements.
- *High salaries.* P.E.s often earn higher salaries than nonlicensed engineers.
- *P.E. title.* P.E.s can sign and seal documents and legally represent themselves to the public as "professional engineers."
- *Career advantages.* Only P.E.s are eligible to work legally as engineering consultants.

Licensing Requirements

It takes several years to become a P.E. The length of time actually varies from state to state as well as individual to individual. However, all registered or licensed engineers have gone through three phases to achieve this designation.

- *Stage 1.* Every P.E. is a graduate of an ABET-accredited engineering program.

- *Stage 2.* Every P.E. has passed the Fundamentals of Engineering (FE) exam. This was formerly called the Engineering-In-Training (EIT) exam. If you see references to the EIT exam, it is the same thing as the FE exam. This is an engineering and science fundamentals test.
- *Stage 3.* After several years of engineering experience, every P.E. has passed the Principles of Practice of Engineering (PE) exam. This is a test of knowledge in a specific branch of engineering (i.e., civil engineering, electrical engineering, etc.). The PE exam tests the engineer's ability to apply engineering principles and judgment to professional problems.

Tips for Meeting the Licensing Requirements

If you think that you will eventually want, or need, to become a licensed engineer, you must make sure that the college or university that you attend has an ABET-accredited engineering program. You need to be careful when selecting your program of study. Some departments or programs within a college or university can be ABET accredited, while others are not. Lists of ABET-accredited engineering schools and specific engineering programs are available by writing to the Accreditation Board for Engineering and Technology (abet.org).

The next step in the licensing process will be passing the Fundamentals of Engineering (FE) exam, formerly the EIT exam. It is administered every fall and spring by state engineering registration boards.

The Chair of the Engineering Deans Council of the American Society for Engineering Education recently stated that engineering students benefited in the long run if they took the FE exam before graduation. This is sound advice when you consider how much knowledge you accumulate as an undergraduate. Two or three years after graduation, it can be extremely difficult to recall concepts and facts necessary to pass the FE exam.

All state boards of registration administer the same FE examination. The exam is produced by the NCEE. However, the dates that the exams are administered can vary slightly from state to state. It is necessary to apply to take the exam well in advance.

Engineering students are advised to take the exam during their senior year in college. Therefore, it is recommended that the semester or quarter prior to starting your senior year in college you contact the engineering registration board in the state or states where you plan to become licensed (see the NCEE website at ncees.org for a list of state engineering registration boards). They will be able to tell you when and where the FE exam will be administered during your senior year and what the application deadline will be.

The FE exam consists of two four-hour periods. The morning exam tests comprehension and knowledge as well as evaluation, analysis, and application. The afternoon exam is composed of problem sets from seven subject areas: statics, dynamics, mechanics of materials, fluid mechanics, electrical theory, and economic analysis.

The FE exam is an open-book test. However, states do vary in the amount of material that you are allowed to bring into the exam. This is important information to ask about when you contact the state board of registration regarding test dates and deadlines.

The third step in the process of becoming a licensed engineer is fulfilling your state's requirements for years of professional experience. The minimum number of years of professional engineering experience is two. However, this requirement varies from state to state.

It is important to know that in some cases your participation in a university-sponsored co-op program may count toward this experience. The semesters or quarters that you co-op (work) will be documented on your academic transcript for review by the registration board.

Finally, you will need to pass the PE exam. This exam will test your in-depth knowledge of a specific field of engineering. If you are a mechanical engineer, the exam you take will test your ability to apply mechanical engineering principles to real-life problems. Likewise, if you are a chemical engineer, you will be tested on the engineering principles in that discipline.

ADDITIONAL INFORMATION

Further information on preparing for a career in engineering is available from the following organizations:

National Council of Examiners for Engineering
P.O. Box 1686
Clemson, SC 29633-1686
ncees.org

Accreditation Board for Engineering and Technology
111 Market Place, Suite 1050
Baltimore, MD 21202-4012
abet.org

CHAPTER 3

FINANCING YOUR ENGINEERING EDUCATION

Cost alone should not deter you from obtaining an engineering education. While you and your family are expected to meet some of the costs of higher education, there are financial assistance programs to help you make the dream of an engineering degree a reality.

The college or university of your choice will have a financial aid representative on staff whose sole responsibility is to assist students in making application for all of the available aid programs for which they qualify. These representatives can assist you in filling out the various forms and will answer your questions concerning the types and amounts of assistance available.

It is very important to understand the differences among the five types of aid available. This aid can take the form of:

- Scholarships
- Grants
- Loans
- Work-study jobs
- Co-op

SCHOLARSHIPS

A scholarship is a monetary grant to a student who qualifies under a variety of circumstances. There are scholarships for the academically gifted.

Other scholarships are based on special abilities such as musical talent, athletics, speech, and drama. Occasionally, the scholarship may have one or more conditions that must be met in terms of academic ability and/or financial need.

The key point to remember is that a scholarship is a grant, or gift, of money for a specific purpose (education) with specific requirements (talent, academic merit, and/or financial need). It does not require repayment. Each institution has its own requirements and qualifications for scholarships. In addition, there are community organizations, businesses, and professional associations that award scholarships to engineering students. A list of engineering associations that offer scholarships is included in Appendix B.

GRANTS

A grant is a gift of financial aid for a specific purpose (education). Like a scholarship, it may impose conditions on the recipient and does not require repayment. Sources of grants include the institution itself; local, state, and federal government; and private industry and groups. Each grant has specific conditions and requirements that must be met.

LOANS

A loan is not a grant or a scholarship. It is a legal obligation that must be repaid. A student loan can be obtained from the learning institution, from a bank or savings and loan, or from a government agency. The government agency's role is usually limited to insuring or guaranteeing the lender—the school, a bank, or a savings and loan—that you will repay the loan according to the terms of the contract.

Certain loans, especially those earmarked for students in high-demand, low-supply career fields, often have special clauses permitting portions of the loan to be cancelled if conditions are met. An example is a loan made to an engineering student who co-ops with a federal agency. According to one such agreement, the loan is cancelled so long as the student works full-time for the agency until the time worked equals the amount of time for which the student received the loan. If the student does not work full-time for the agency, the loan must be repaid with interest.

The important thing to keep in mind is that all loans must be repaid in some manner. Interest charges are almost always added to an educational loan. Repayment usually does not begin until after you have graduated. There are exceptions to this, so ask lots of questions when applying for educational loans.

It is important to remember that if you do not repay the loan, the lender may take legal action against you to ensure that the loan is repaid. If the federal government guarantees your loan, and you fail to pay, then legally your income tax refund checks and your wages can be garnished until the debt is satisfied.

APPLYING FOR FINANCIAL AID

Schools use a confidential statement of income and assets from parents and student to determine what financial aid a student is eligible for. If the student is independent and does not live at home with his or her parents, then the application will reflect information about the student alone. If you fall under this category, you might want to discuss the options available to you with the financial aid representative before proceeding any further.

Application forms and the confidential statement of assets and income can vary from one school to another. You should determine exactly which forms the school of your choice requires and be certain to submit only those forms. The forms have a deadline for submission, so you should be sure that you have the forms and collect the information in plenty of time to meet this deadline.

Questions on the application will assess the financial condition of the family unit. From your responses, the financial aid committee can determine an estimate of how much money your family can reasonably be expected to contribute toward your education and how much outside assistance you will require.

This assessment will take into account your family's size, income, assets and liabilities, and the number of family members attending postsecondary educational facilities. Your parents' ages and the resources available to you will also enter into the final analysis.

A standard formula is used to ensure that all students are considered in an impartial manner. Your financial aid administrator should be made aware of any special family circumstances that should be considered in this formula along with the information solicited on the application. This special information should be detailed in a letter, which should be sent with any supporting documentation to the aid representative.

HOW MUCH WILL MY EDUCATION COST?

What a college degree costs depends on the type of institution you select. Private Ivy League colleges usually cost a great deal more than local, state-supported colleges. Each school will, on request, provide you with a breakdown of its student expenses. This budget consists of the following items:

- *Tuition and fees.* This represents the amount you will be charged for your classes.
- *Books and supplies.* This will vary based on the type of academic program you have selected. Be sure to ask about special books or equipment (lab supplies and computers) required of students in your program.
- *Housing.* This amount will reflect either rates for available housing on campus (dorms) or, if no housing is available, the prevailing rents in the local community.
- *Meals.* If there is a school cafeteria, the amount will be somewhat fixed. If you must eat out, the cost can vary substantially. Sometimes a fixed board fee will also include laundry and telephone and computer hookups. Be sure to ask.
- *Personal expenses.* This is your allowance, an amount of money for entertainment, personal items, and miscellaneous charges you might incur.
- *Transportation.* This is an allowance for trips from school back to your home, for example.

While these costs can vary, especially if you elect to live at home and attend a local college, these factors must be considered to determine what your college education will really cost. You might want to fill out the following chart to help you determine the basic costs.

Estimating the Cost of Your Education

Tuition and fees	_____
Books and supplies	_____
Room/housing	_____
Board/meals	_____
Personal expenses	_____
Transportation	_____
Other expenses	_____
Total estimated college cost	_____
Estimated family contribution	_____
Estimated aid requirement (subtract estimated family contribution from total estimated college cost)	_____
Total	_____

HOW WILL I KNOW WHAT AID I'LL RECEIVE?

The financial aid office at your school will notify you of its decision in what is called an award letter or award notification form. This will tell you what kind or kinds of aid you can expect and the amounts for which you are eligible.

This will cover all of the available forms of aid you have qualified for, including scholarships, grants, student employment, and loans. Many institutions call this award a financial aid package.

After you have received this letter, you should notify the financial aid representative that you either accept or decline the aid. Some schools will withdraw the offer of assistance if you do not notify them by a specified deadline.

WORK-STUDY JOBS AND CO-OP

Although these two forms of assistance do not fall under the traditional categories, they may be available to you even if you do not qualify for any other assistance. The work-study job assigns you to a specific job, usually on campus, and pays you for every hour you work. This can be used to supplement scholarships and grants as long as you ensure that your work schedule does not conflict with your education.

A co-op position can add at least a year to your college life, but it can be of substantial benefit and actually put you ahead of students who were able to attend school full-time. You are assigned to a company where you will work in an area closely related to your chosen profession. You work certain periods of time and attend school during other periods of time. In doing so, you will gain valuable experience in your field that can make a financial difference when you graduate and pursue your first job. In addition, it may be possible for you to graduate less in debt because engineering salaries, including co-op salaries, tend to be higher than average.

Remember, there is no reason not to get an engineering education. Financial aid programs and scholarships can help you afford the cost of higher education.

CHAPTER 4

WOMEN IN ENGINEERING

Engineering has no gender. It requires an interest and ability in the physical sciences and mathematics as well as in problem solving. Both men and women have these abilities and interests. People who succeed in engineering have a strong commitment to applying scientific and engineering principles to the needs of societies. While women are still underrepresented in engineering, there is a strong need for them to contribute to solving some of the pressing problems of our times.

STATISTICS ON WOMEN IN ENGINEERING

Currently, women represent only 13 to 15 percent of all engineering graduates. From the late 1960s until the early 1980s, the number of women receiving degrees in science and engineering steadily increased. However, in the mid to late 1980s the number of women receiving degrees in these areas began to decrease.

Studies have shown that the high school years are critical in preparing for a career in engineering. This is particularly true for women and for other underrepresented groups in engineering. It is important for high school women to know what the requirements are for entering college engineering programs. This information is vital when making decisions about what courses to take and which activities to pursue in high school.

The preceding chapters demonstrate that math and physical sciences are basic requirements for every engineering major. Yet a study at the University of Michigan found that women in high school continue to take fewer mathematics and science courses than do men. This phenomenon is not due to lack of ability on the part of high school women but, in many cases, it is due to lack of adequate information about the need for these courses in many college majors—particularly in engineering.

However, high school preparation in math and science does not fully account for the different rates of participation of women and men in engineering. Factors such as self-confidence; stereotypes about women in engineering; encouragement from family, teachers, counselors, and friends; and opportunities for hands-on experiences related to science and engineering play key roles in whether or not a young woman decides to pursue a career in engineering.

ADVICE TO WOMEN ENTERING ENGINEERING

A bachelor's degree in engineering will provide the basic preparation for many exciting opportunities in engineering. However, there are other skills that will greatly facilitate one's success in the field of engineering. These skills fall into four categories: writing, public speaking, teamwork, and getting the job done.

The most important of these career skills is writing ability. Generally, engineers are not known for their writing ability. However, you will need to be able to communicate your work and proposals. Reports, memos, letters, and proposals will be read and evaluated by audiences such as management, clients, peers, and so on.

Learning to tighten your writing so that your ideas are clear and concise will be extremely important. Annual reports, expert testimony, responses to dissatisfied customers, and replies to regulatory agencies are some of the types of writing that will demand versatile writing skills.

The second skill is public speaking. It is often said that public speaking is not an optional skill for engineers. Presentations are a standard part of the engineering workplace. Sometimes these speeches are impromptu. Speaking is important because various groups will need to be sold on the business and technical merit of your projects.

Avoiding opportunities to speak will not help improve your skills in this area. Therefore, it is important to join groups and/or take public speaking courses to improve your speaking ability. Joining a local Toastmasters group is an excellent method of improving public speaking.

The third area is teamwork. Too often engineers can take an "engineering only" outlook. It is easy for engineers to see only the technical aspects of their work. However, it is important for engineers to look at the broader issues that are facing their companies or organizations.

American industry is increasingly taking a team approach to solving problems. The teams usually are made up of people from diverse disciplines within the organization. The teams may consist of a marketing person, an accountant, legal counsel, and an engineer. These cross-functional teams work together to solve a problem or develop a new product. Women engineers need the skills to be active and productive members of these teams.

Finally, it is important to get the job done. Women engineers who are entering the workforce for the first time need to understand that the work environment and the classroom environment differ greatly. Work assignments can overlap and instructions are not always clear and definitive.

Knowing what it takes to successfully get your job done is something that is not taught in the classroom. Incorporating hands-on experience, such as cooperative engineering education (co-op), in your college career can ease the transition from school to work because you will learn to work in an environment that provides support and encouragement. You will learn to ask for help, to meet deadlines, and to perform as a professional engineer in industry before you graduate from college. This type of learning is invaluable to the new engineer.

In addition to developing skills beyond their technical expertise, women in engineering need to be prepared to learn from one another. This can be accomplished through networking and mentoring programs. Whether these programs are formal or informal, they help women "learn the ropes" and further their personal and career development. Knowing your industry and being active in your field of engineering will expand opportunities for advancement.

ORGANIZATIONS FOR WOMEN IN ENGINEERING

Association for Women in Computing (AWC)
41 Sutter Street, Suite 1006
San Francisco, CA 94104
awc-hq.org

National Association of Women in Construction (NAWIC)
327 South Adams Street
Fort Worth, TX 76104
nawic.org

Society of Women Engineers (SWE)
230 East Ohio Street, Suite 400
Chicago, IL 60611-3265
swe.org

CHAPTER

5

MINORITIES IN ENGINEERING

Did you know that the innovative body design of the Saturn SL I automobile was the responsibility of an African-American engineer? Did you know that the manager of research at one of IBM's major research laboratories is an Hispanic engineer? Did you know that another major research laboratory, which receives money from the University of California and the U.S. Department of Energy, has an American Indian Program and a joint engineering pact with the Navajos?

STATISTICS ON MINORITIES IN ENGINEERING

While these achievements are significant, they do not mean that minorities have achieved equality in the field of engineering. Minorities represent approximately 22 percent of our total society. There are over fifty-four million African-Americans, Hispanics, American Indians, and Alaskan natives. However, these groups are underrepresented in engineering. According to the National Action Council for Minorities in Engineering, the trend for minorities in engineering is up. However, representation for all minority groups except Asian-Americans is still well below their proportions in the general public.

LeRoy Callender, P.E., president of LeRoy Callender PC Consulting Engineers based in New York, offered a partial explanation for the underrepresentation of African-Americans. "A few years ago, there weren't many

Blacks majoring in engineering because it didn't make sense to work hard for a degree and not be able to get a job. Now, a Black engineer is worth his/her weight in gold."

The Council on Competitiveness would agree with Mr. Callender. The council estimated that the United States would have a shortage of five hundred thousand engineers and scientists. This shortage is the result of too few people in the engineering education "pipeline." Consequently, more and more companies target minority engineering students for scholarships and permanent job offers after graduation. In other words, Mr. Callender's assessment of the current opportunities for minority engineers is correct!

A more serious barrier to minorities entering engineering careers is inadequate educational preparation. When students do not take a sufficient amount of math and physical science during middle and high school, they have an educational lack when it comes to selecting engineering as a college major.

ADVICE FOR MINORITY ENGINEERS

If you plan to pursue a career in engineering, it is important to be prepared. During high school you need to take as much mathematics and science as possible. This means that you should take calculus and trigonometry in addition to the usual algebra and geometry. You also need to take courses in biology, chemistry, and physics, including advanced courses in chemistry and physics. Most high schools offer advanced placement (AP) courses in math and science. If you plan to pursue an engineering major in college it is strongly advised that you take these AP courses. These courses will prepare you for the basic educational requirements for most engineering majors.

With the right educational tools and a strong desire to achieve, anyone can make an impact. However, minorities in engineering have had few role models or mentors. Therefore, finding support for your interest in engineering is very important.

Your family, your teachers, and your guidance counselors are people who can possibly help you identify individuals, organizations, and local industries knowledgeable about engineering and willing to be supportive of your interest in engineering. In addition to these groups, contact the organizations listed at the end of this chapter, and at the end of each chapter that discusses an engineering field in which you are interested.

Organizations such as the National Society of Black Engineers (NSBE) and the Society for Hispanic Professional Engineers (SHPE) seek to identify minority students and encourage them to pursue education and employment in engineering. These organizations offer tutoring programs, group study sessions, junior and senior high school outreach programs, technical seminars and workshops, a national communications network, résumé books, career fairs, summer jobs, and so on. Their support and encouragement will help you launch and pursue a successful career in engineering.

Local industry, business, and government agencies that employ engineers will also be happy to assist you in meeting engineers and showing you what engineers do in their setting. Often a phone call to the human resources department can be very helpful in setting up such a meeting.

Selecting an engineering school will be an important step in your engineering career. When evaluating colleges and universities, it is not only important to examine the curriculum and learn about the faculty, it is also important to meet members of the local chapters of NSBE, SHPE, and other minority engineering organizations on campus. Many chapters are extremely active and provide a strong support network for their members. Make sure the schools you are looking at have strong chapters of this type of organization.

During your college career it is also important to gain hands-on experience related to engineering. This may be through summer work experience, but in college it is important to take a serious look at cooperative engineering education (co-op) programs.

Co-op is a well-known educational approach for engineers, and hundreds of thousands of engineers have graduated from colleges with co-op experience. Co-op is the type of hands-on experience on which industry places a very high value. Many major corporations that recruit engineers make permanent job offers to their co-op students first. Therefore, it will be increasingly important for minority engineering students to participate in co-op programs so that they are assured of being part of this pool of highly sought-after job candidates for permanent employment.

You and your family should talk to the staff of the co-op office at any college or university that you are considering attending. Sometimes there can be a misconception that college co-op programs are not for the serious academic student. This is far from the truth. Co-op employers are seeking the best and the brightest, and they have a vested interest in their co-op students receiving their degrees. A reputable co-op program will not continue to work with employers who hire students away from the classroom. Therefore, it is important for you and your family to visit the co-op office and ask lots of questions.

ORGANIZATIONS FOR MINORITY ENGINEERS

National Society of Black Engineers (NSBE)
1454 Duke Street
Alexandria, VA 22314
nsbe.org

National Society of Black Physicists (NSBP)
6704G Lee Highway
Arlington, VA 22205
http://nsbp.org

International Society of African Scientists (ISAS)
P.O. Box 9209
Wilmington, DE 19809
dca.net/isas

American Indian Science and Engineering Society (AISES)
P.O. Box 9828
Albuquerque, NM 87119-9828
aises.org

Society of Hispanic Professional Engineers (SHPE)
5400 East Olympic Boulevard, Suite 210
Los Angeles, CA 90022
shpe.org

Society for Advancement of Chicanos and Native Americans in Science
    (SACNAS)
P.O. Box 8526
Santa Cruz, CA 95061-8526
sacnas.org

Society of Mexican American Engineers and Scientists (MAES)
maes-natl.org

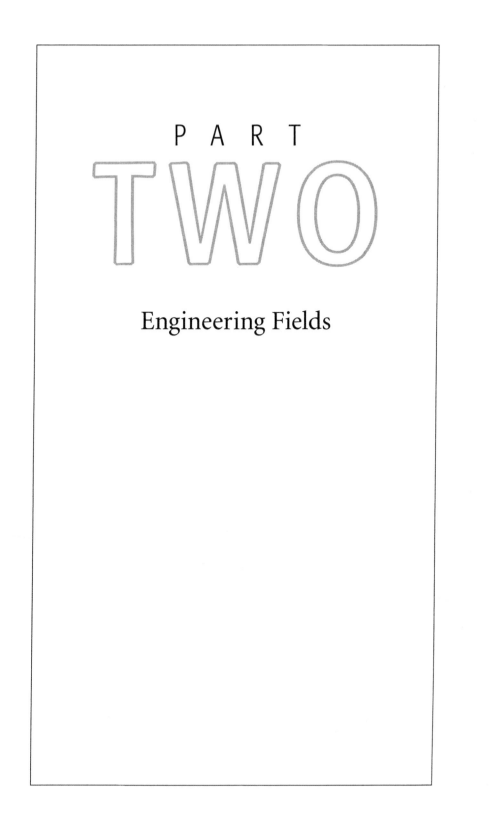

P A R T

TWO

Engineering Fields

C H A P T E R

6

CHEMICAL ENGINEERING

While chemists are interested in the basic composition of elements and compounds found in nature, and some seek to invent new products from them, chemical engineers work to develop new products and to evaluate them practically and economically. As a result, chemical engineering is one of the oldest and most established engineering fields. However, there are fewer chemical engineers than any other group of engineers. Therefore, they are highly sought by industry because their impact is significant, particularly in the past century.

Consider some of the chemical engineering contributions that have literally changed our lives. Chemical engineers have split the atom; developed catalytic cracking to form products such as gasoline, plastics, and synthetic rubbers and fibers; and improved the environment through catalytic converters and recycling technologies.

It is the chemical engineer who takes raw materials and turns them into new technologies and products that we use every day. The jackets and shoes that we wear are most likely the result of innovations in synthetic fibers that chemical engineering has made possible. Likewise, stain-resistant seat covers in our cars and stain-resistant rugs in our homes are also the work of chemical engineers.

Chemical engineers combine the science of chemistry with the discipline of engineering to solve a wide range of technical problems such as finding more efficient ways of producing things such as plastics, synthetic rubber, medications, food, petrochemicals, and artificial organs. The work of chemical engineers has contributed greatly to the quality of life that we enjoy today.

It has been said that chemical engineering is the most versatile of all the engineering disciplines. As a result, those who prepare to be chemical engineers are able to handle a wide range of technical problems. They are involved in every phase of the complex production of chemicals and chemical by-products.

THE NATURE OF THE WORK

As stated earlier, chemical engineers turn raw materials into useful products. In order to do this, chemical engineers know how to design new chemical compounds and chemical processes. They also know how to test new compounds and products to assure such things as their quality, durability, and manufacturability.

Today, chemical engineers use specialized computer technology for the chemical engineering field. They use this knowledge in their research as well as in the production of chemicals and chemical by-products. Chemical engineers also use computer skills to control automated systems in chemical plants and in manufacturing plants. Computer software skills are very necessary for chemical engineers who conduct analysis of research data gathered while developing new products and systems.

In combining the science of chemistry with the discipline of engineering, chemical engineers work with such problems as:

- Producing more effective pharmaceuticals and medical devices
- Producing safer cosmetics
- Developing more efficient methods of refining petroleum
- Purifying polluted water and air
- Developing more durable and versatile products such as plastics and synthetic rubber and fiber
- Harnessing solar and geothermal sources of energy
- Recycling reusable metals, glass, and plastics
- Producing cheaper and better fertilizers and pesticides
- Creating more effective paints, dyes, and coatings
- Manufacturing improved electronics and semiconductors

- Producing paper and pulp products
- Producing nutritional and convenient food products

To understand the nature of the work of chemical engineers in one company, let's look at Kraft Foods. Chemical engineers at Kraft Foods can be involved in five different areas of research and development (R&D).

Some chemical engineers are involved in *research*. That means that they develop technology to improve existing Kraft products or to explore the possibility of new products.

Some are involved in *product development*. That means that they improve current Kraft products and develop the new products that research engineers tell them are possible.

Some are involved in *process research and development*. That means that they develop methods to change raw materials into finished Kraft products.

Some are involved in *package research and development*. That means that they use their knowledge of package design to make sure that Kraft packaging will keep food products fresher longer and that the packaging is environmentally safe.

Some are involved in *quality and safety*. That means that they put safety requirements in place for both Kraft workers and Kraft customers. And because Kraft produces food that people will eat, the chemical engineers who work in this area also make sure that Kraft meets all the requirements of the U.S. Food and Drug Administration and other government agencies, such as the Environmental Protection Agency, that help to regulate the food industry.

As seen in the Kraft Foods example, chemical engineers perform many different functions, even if it is in just one of the areas in which chemical engineers work. The areas in which chemical engineers typically work include research and development, design and construction, operations and production, technical sales, and environmental and waste management. Each area is described below.

Research and Development

Research and development (R&D) is an area in which chemical engineers spend much of their time designing and performing experiments and interpreting the data obtained. They may invent and create new and better ways of developing products, controlling pollution, reducing safety and health hazards, and conserving natural resources. Their findings may be refined in laboratories, but more often are tested in a pilot plant, which is a miniature version of the proposed commercial facility.

Some R&D, such as that conducted by Kraft Foods, is done in the company itself. Other chemical engineering research is conducted in universities. This research is conducted under the direction of chemical engineering faculty members, with the assistance of graduate and undergraduate students. In all cases, research is aimed at technology development and a better understanding of the different ways in which chemicals can interact under various conditions.

Design and Construction

Design and construction is another area in which chemical engineers work. These engineers are known as project engineers. They design and construct chemical manufacturing facilities. They may work directly for a manufacturing firm or for a consulting company hired by the manufacturer.

In design work, chemical engineers draw heavily on their knowledge of mathematics, physics, chemistry, and other related sciences. They use this knowledge to select and size equipment and determine the optimum method of production. Chemical engineers design computerized control systems to maintain consistent product quality, minimize waste generation, and assure safe operation of the facility. They develop capital and operating costs and present anticipated profitability statements to justify the proposed project. After the project is accepted, they prepare detailed specifications, drawings, and priority schedules.

Chemical engineers in design and construction may act as field engineers, directing and assisting workers during the construction period. After construction, these engineers may assist in installing and testing new equipment, as well as training equipment operators. The most experienced chemical engineers will usually be the people responsible for actually starting up the plant and making sure that everything works as planned.

Operations and Production

Operations and production is another area in which chemical engineers work. Chemical engineers in operations are responsible for the day-to-day operation of a manufacturing facility. Their primary interest is in the production of a product economically and safely in order to meet the customers' needs in both quality and quantity. They are challenged by raw material variations and shortages, labor disruption, cost fluctuations, weather, and equipment breakdowns. They gradually adjust operating conditions to achieve improved product yield and quality and reduced operating costs.

Technical Sales

Technical sales is another area in which chemical engineers work. Chemical engineers involved in technical sales not only have strong technical skills, they also have exceptional people skills. It is their responsibility to introduce new products to customers and to assess why some products do better than others in the marketplace. In the area of total quality management, chemical engineers involved in technical sales provide a vital link in determining why a given product is not functioning to a customer's satisfaction.

Environmental and Waste Management

Environmental and waste management is another area in which chemical engineers work. Chemical engineers employed in this area devise techniques to recover usable materials from waste products and develop methods to reduce the pollution created during the manufacturing of a product. They also design waste storage and treatment facilities, as well as design pollution-control strategies for plant operations.

It is obvious now that chemical engineers do not work in isolation. Their work requires strong engineering skills as well as good skills in dealing with all types of people. They have to work with people from different disciplines and from different areas of the company to accomplish their job. Chemical engineers not only have to be technically competent, but they also have to be able to communicate with people who work in such areas as marketing, accounting, sales, and information systems, as well as other engineering groups. This combination makes chemical engineering very rewarding!

THE SETTINGS IN WHICH CHEMICAL ENGINEERS WORK

While approximately 30 percent of chemical engineers work in consulting and government service, the majority of chemical engineers work in manufacturing industries. The largest of these industries is the chemical industry. Because the primary concern of chemical engineers is large-scale manufacture of products from raw materials through closely controlled physical and chemical changes, they find employment in such diverse areas of the chemical industry as agricultural chemicals, plastics, and industrial chemicals.

The petroleum industry is another that employs many chemical engineers. However, in recent years, chemical engineers have found themselves in demand by electronics, photographic equipment, pulp and paper, pharmaceutical, biomedical, cosmetic, and food-processing industries.

Other emerging industries for chemical engineers include atomic energy development and coal conversion. However, the fastest-growing areas for chemical engineers are the pharmaceutical, electronics, and environmental industries. Government agencies such as the U.S. Department of Energy, the Food and Drug Administration, and the Environmental Protection Agency also employ a large number of chemical engineers.

Chemical engineers work in local, state, and federal government agencies to advise lawmakers on environmental issues and industrial concerns. They develop laws and standards to protect the environment and the public from chemical hazards.

In addition to these areas, there are others. For example, almost one-third of the chemical engineers in the United States function as managers and supervisors and have become removed from day-to-day chemical engineering responsibilities. Others work for consulting firms, and still others teach chemical engineering at colleges and universities.

EDUCATION AND OTHER QUALIFICATIONS

Education for chemical engineering begins in junior high school with the appropriate math and science courses to prepare for three years of high school science, including chemistry and physics, and four years of mathematics through trigonometry or calculus. In high school it is also necessary to take at least three years of English.

While the course work required for a bachelor's degree in chemical engineering may vary slightly from school to school, the American Institute of Chemical Engineers (AIChE), states that undergraduate chemical engineering programs must include classes that provide a strong knowledge of:

- General chemistry
- Advanced chemistry (e.g., organic, inorganic, physical, analytical, and materials chemistry, as well as biochemistry)
- Materials and energy balances applied to chemical processes (including safety and environmental aspects)
- Thermodynamics of physical and chemical equilibria
- Heat, mass, and momentum transfer
- Chemical reaction engineering
- Continuous and stage-wise separation operations
- Process dynamics and control
- Process design
- Modern experimental and computing techniques

Examine the course requirements in chemical engineering described on the websites of the seven different colleges and universities nationwide listed below to see the similarities and differences at each institution:

- University of Arizona
  (engr.arizona.edu/~acadaff/curricula/014/chem.html)
- University of Florida (reg.ufl.edu/01-02-catalog/colleges/engineering/programs-chemical.html)
- University of Michigan
  (engin.umich.edu/dept/cheme/ugoffice/degreq.html)
- University of Massachusetts, Amherst
  (ecs.umass.edu/che/che_web/ug_table.html)
- Virginia Tech University
  (che.vt.edu/Ugradprogram/curriculum.pdf)
- University of Southern California
  (usc.edu/dept/publications/cat2001/engineering)

• University of Oklahoma (ou.edu/bulletins/degree-sheets/engr/engrindx.htm)

For a list of other ABET-accredited chemical engineering programs, go to aiche.org/education/abet.htm.

Chemical engineering careers in business, industry, and government require a minimum of a bachelor's degree in chemical engineering. Positions in teaching or research require additional college education at the master's and Ph.D. levels. Regardless of the work setting, chemical engineers need to continually update their knowledge and skills through continuing education courses and/or advanced degrees in order to remain current in their field.

OUTLOOK FOR THE FUTURE

The continued demand for new and improved products and more economical processes will assure a steady demand for chemical engineers. However, government projections indicate that the number of openings for chemical engineers in manufacturing will be lower. In the manufacturing sector, the best opportunities will most likely be in the areas of specialty chemicals, plastics, materials, pharmaceuticals, and electronics.

Nonmanufacturing opportunities for chemical engineers are expected to grow. This means that consulting firms, government agencies, and academic settings will continue to seek chemical engineers. Therefore, as in the past, there will always be a need for chemical engineers.

EARNINGS

In 2001, the National Association of Colleges and Employers reported that bachelor's-degree graduates in chemical engineering received starting offers averaging $51,073 annually. Master's-degree candidates averaged $57,221, and Ph.D. candidates averaged $75,521.

Chemical engineers who were already employed in the field had a median income of $65,960 in 2000, according to the U.S. Bureau of Labor Statistics. This means that half of the employed chemical engineers in 2000 made more than $65,960 a year and half made less. Only 10 percent of chemical engineers earned less than $45,200, and 10 percent earned more than $93,430.

ADDITIONAL SOURCES OF INFORMATION

American Chemical Society (ACS)
1155 Sixteenth Street NW
Washington, DC 20036
acs.org

American Institute of Chemical Engineers
3 Park Avenue
New York, NY 10016-5991
aiche.org/careers

American Petroleum Institute (API)
1220 L Street NW
Washington, DC 20005
api.org

Independent Petroleum Association of America (IPAA)
1101 Sixteenth Street NW
Washington, DC 20036
ipaa.org

Society of Petroleum Engineers
P.O. Box 833836
Richardson, TX 75083-3836
spe.org

Society of Plastics Engineers (SPE)
14 Fairfield Drive
Brookfield, CT 06804-0403
4spe.org

CHAPTER

7

CIVIL ENGINEERING*

Civil engineering is widely recognized as the oldest and broadest of the engineering disciplines. From the pyramids of Egypt to the exploration of space, civil engineers have always faced the challenges of the future—advancing civilization and building our quality of life. Today, civil engineers continue to design and build the infrastructure—bridges, highways, rail and water systems, etc.—that supports almost every facet of our lives, meeting the challenges of pollution, traffic congestion, drinking water and energy needs, urban redevelopment, and community planning. To accomplish this they must be in the forefront of technology, making civil engineers frequent users of sophisticated high-tech products, particularly the very latest concepts in computer-aided design (CAD).

Civil engineers offer the world answers and supply solutions for both new and existing problems. For example, earthquake codes were developed, in part, by civil engineers striving to improve public safety. Wind hazard codes are currently being researched and strengthened to ensure a safer quality of life for inhabitants of wind-risk areas. In 1995, civil engineers examined the blast damage of the Murrah Federal Building in Oklahoma City, to assure that new federal construction reflects the lessons learned from this tragedy. Today, civil engineers are looking at how the buildings performed during the September 11, 2001, tragedies at the World Trade

---

*Content contributed by the American Society of Civil Engineering.

Center towers and the Pentagon, searching to make our world more secure in the face of new hazards.

The profession extends across many technical areas, and civil engineering specialties interact with one another on a variety of projects and issues. Regardless of specialty area, civil engineers share a common denominator: *civil engineers are problem-solvers who help people*. They are responsible for serving their communities by improving the quality of life. Service to people and, specifically, to the development and improvement of the communities in which we all live sums up what civil engineers do.

THE NATURE OF THE WORK

Civil engineers are involved in the conception, planning, design, construction, and management of projects essential to modern life, ranging from transit systems to offshore structures, such as oil platforms, to space satellites. Therefore, they may alternately find themselves at a computer workstation, in front of a public hearing, or on a project work site. Most civil engineers routinely work as part of a team that may include other engineers, scientists, contractors, project owners, architects, bankers, lawyers, and government officials.

According to the American Society of Civil Engineers (ASCE), the oldest national professional engineering organization in the country, there are several specialties within civil engineering. These include structural engineering, urban planning and construction engineering, environmental engineering, transportation and pipeline engineering, and geotechnical engineering.

Structural Engineering

The structural engineer faces the challenge of analyzing and designing structures to ensure that they safely perform their purpose. Stadiums, arenas, skyscrapers, offshore oil structures, space platforms, amusement park rides, bridges, office buildings, and homes are some of the projects in which structural engineers are involved. These structures must support their own weight and resist dynamic environmental loads such as hurricanes, earthquakes, fires, blizzards, blasts, and floods.

Taking these variables into consideration, the engineer determines a combination of appropriate building materials that can include steel, concrete, wood, and other materials. If a structure must support a load and is made from steel, aluminum, concrete, or other materials, the structural engineer will ensure the correct combination of these materials is used to safely support the load. To make certain that the plans are being followed, structural engineers are often on the construction site inspecting and verifying the work.

Structural engineers are team players. They normally work with architects, mechanical and electrical engineers, contractors, representatives of project owners, lawyers, public officials, and financial specialists.

Urban Planning and Construction Engineering

Urban engineers (planners) are concerned with the full development of a community. Urban planners use both technical and managerial skills to analyze the variety of information needed to coordinate projects, such as projecting street patterns, identifying park and recreation areas, and determining areas for industrial and residential growth.

The construction phase of a project represents the first tangible results of a design. Using their technical and management skills, construction engineers help turn designs into reality by applying their knowledge of construction methods and equipment, along with principles of financing, planning, and managing, to turn the designs of other engineers into successful facilities.

Urban planners and construction engineers team up frequently to build better communities. In urban and community planning, these civil engineers are concerned with the development of the total community. This involves consulting with local authorities on the integration of the community with mass transportation and other related facilities, and bringing the project in on time and within budget.

Environmental Engineering

Environmental engineers design and supervise systems that prevent and control pollution in water, on land, in the air, and in the groundwater supply. Their efforts are critical to all areas of water resource management, including the design of water treatment and distribution systems, wastewater collection, treatment facilities, and the containment of hazardous wastes. In this field, an engineer might be called upon to resolve problems of providing safe drinking water, cleaning up sites contaminated with hazardous materials, cleaning up and preventing air pollution, treating wastewater, protecting beaches, and managing solid waste.

The environmental engineer plays an increasingly important role in providing for the orderly growth of a community as well as for its continued quality of life. This becomes even more important as people move from crowded cities to what was once rural America. As people move to the country, so do industries and jobs. This influx places an increased demand on the public works of a community, so the environmental engineer's role as a planner and facilitator becomes even more important. Through the engineer's management and planning, growth remains orderly as the community expands to meet the growing needs of its citizens. The environmental engineer, by virtue of his or her mission, works closely with the engineers specializing in construction engineering and urban planning.

Transportation and Pipeline Engineering

Transportation engineers are involved with the safe and efficient movement of people, goods, and materials. They design and maintain all types of transportation components, including highways and streets, mass transit systems, railroads and airports, and ports and harbors.

Transportation engineers apply technical knowledge and an understanding of political, economic, and social factors in their projects. They work closely with urban planners and construction engineers, since the quality of the community is directly related to the quality of its transportation system.

The transportation of gas, oil, and other commodities through pipelines has created another civil engineering specialty—the pipeline engineer. This specialty combines knowledge of hydraulics, geotechnical engineering, and the structural properties of pipeline materials to ensure a steady, reliable flow of these vital commodities. Like the transportation engineer, the pipeline engineer works together with the construction engineer, environmental engineer, and urban planner.

Geotechnical Engineering

Almost all of the facilities that make up our infrastructure are in, on, or from earth materials, and geotechnical engineering is the discipline that deals with applications of technology to solve related problems.

Geotechnical engineers analyze the properties of soil and rock that support and affect the behavior of structures, pavements, and underground facilities. In conjunction with environmental engineers, they evaluate the potential settlements of buildings, the stability of slopes and fields, seepage of groundwater, and the effects of earthquakes. With structural and construction engineers, geotechnical engineers take part in the design and construction of earth structures (dams and levees), foundations of buildings, and other construction projects such as offshore platforms, tunnels, and dams.

Geotechnical engineers are also involved in making precise measurements of the earth's surface to obtain reliable information for locating and designing engineering projects. Currently, geotechnical engineers make use of satellites, aerial and terrestrial photomapping, and computer processing of photographic imagery to most efficiently and effectively place and design tunnels, highways, and dams and to plot flood-control and irrigation projects.

Engineering Management

A career in civil engineering can eventually lead to a position in management. In fact, some small-project construction engineers, surveying team supervisors, and assistant municipal engineers are able to start their engineering careers in management.

Positions in management require technical education, the ability to organize and direct workers and materials, and excellent interpersonal skills. As these skills develop, so does the amount of responsibility the civil engineer handles, until eventually he or she manages larger projects that have budgets of millions of dollars. Interpersonal skills, combined with well-developed communication and engineering abilities, can give any engineer a distinct advantage when seeking a management position.

Teaching Civil Engineering

Many civil engineers, after they have earned advanced degrees, share their knowledge and experience as teachers or professors of engineering. Beginning as an assistant professor, an engineer can progress to full professor or head of a department, teaching both undergraduate and graduate students.

Teaching is an especially rewarding way to relay knowledge that has been acquired over the years to prospective civil engineers. Due to their vast experience, faculty members are frequently asked to serve on technical boards, commissions, and other authorities associated with major engineering projects and research initiatives.

THE SETTINGS IN WHICH CIVIL ENGINEERS WORK

In addition to engineering consulting firms, federal, state, and local governments are major employers of civil engineers. Civil engineers also work for utility and oil companies, telecommunication businesses, and even toy and athletic equipment manufacturers. Also, civil engineers often work as consultants in their area of expertise.

The diversity of work and work settings makes civil engineering a dynamic profession. For instance, some civil engineers spend as much as 75 to 80 percent of their time outdoors. There are also opportunities that allow civil engineers to spend most of their time indoors.

EDUCATION AND OTHER QUALIFICATIONS

Entrance into an accredited civil engineering program may be at the freshman level following high school or at the junior level after completing an approved two-year junior college program. The typical four-year program of study in civil engineering includes one year of mathematics and basic sciences; one year of engineering science and analysis; one year of engineering theory and design; and one year that includes social sciences, humanities, communications, and ethics and professionalism, along with electives that complement your overall education.

The specific curriculum offered by different colleges varies. The exact information is listed in college catalogs. A list of accredited civil engineering programs can be obtained from the Accreditation Board for Engineering and Technology (ABET).

A typical civil engineering program might include courses in the following areas:

- *Basic science.* Math, physics, and chemistry
- *Engineering.* Engineering and scientific programming, introduction to engineering, mechanics, soil mechanics, engineering geology, strength of materials, dynamics, analysis of determinate and indeterminate structures, hydraulics, and surveying
- *Engineering design.* Engineering design, design of steel and concrete structures
- *Communications.* English, speech, technical writing, computer languages, and graphics
- *General education.* History, philosophy, psychology, sociology, anthropology, art, music, and literature

OUTLOOK FOR THE FUTURE

Since the beginning of World War II, technological change in the United States has taken place at an ever-increasing rate. This rapid pace has produced changes in the style and standard of living throughout the world, particularly the United States and Western Europe. Stronger emphasis and dependence on technology and infrastructure has in turn produced an increased need for engineers.

While there are always shifts in engineering priorities that cause periodic changes in the demand for a given engineering field, there has always been a steady need for civil engineering graduates. There is very little likelihood that this demand will ever disappear. The types of activities in which civil engineers are engaged are critical to the continuing maintenance and improvement of quality of life everywhere. Civil engineers focus on creating the infrastructure that surrounds and supports us. These activities range from the most fundamental, such as the supply of clean and pure drinking water, to the most sophisticated, such as the construction of space stations. The bottom line is that employment prospects for civil engineers have always been good in the past and, because there is a necessity for civil-engineered resources in each person's daily life, they will likely become even better.

The infrastructure of our country is currently a high priority of business and government. Without a strong infrastructure, the economy cannot grow and expand. This realization and a need to rebuild and refurbish our roads, bridges, and buildings is creating a new demand for civil engineers.

EARNINGS

According to the National Society of Professional Engineers Income and Salary Survey 2001, the median salary for civil engineers is approximately $73,000 annually. Salaries in 2001 ranged from $46,000 to more than $135,000 annually.

ADDITIONAL SOURCES OF INFORMATION

American Society of Civil Engineering (ASCE)
1801 Alexander Bell Drive
Reston, VA 20191
asce.org
ASCE institutes (asce.org/inst_found):
Architectural Engineering Institute (AEI)
Construction Institute (CI)
The Coasts, Oceans, Ports and Rivers Institute (COPRI)
Environmental and Water Resources Institute (EWRI)
Geo-Institute (GI)
Structural Engineering Institute (SEI)

American Association of State Highway and Transportation Officials
    (AASHTO)
444 North Capital Street NW, Suite 249
Washington, DC 20001
aashto.org

American Congress of Surveying and Mapping (ACSM)
6 Montgomery Village Avenue, Suite 403
Gaithersburg, MD 20879
acsm.net

American Concrete Institute (ACI)
P.O. Box 9094
Farmington Hills, MI 48333
aci-int.org

American Concrete Pipe Association (ACPA)
222 Las Colinas Boulevard West, Suite 641
Irving, TX 75039-5423
concrete-pipe.org

American Council of Engineering Companies
1015 Fifteenth Street NW
Washington, DC 20005
acec.org
Coalitions and special interest groups:
Council of American Structural Engineers (CASE)
Council of Professional Surveyors (COPS)
Design Professionals Coalition (DPC)
Environmental Business Action Coalition (EBAC)
Research Management Foundation (RMF)
Small Firm Council (SFC)

American Underground Construction Association (AUA)
511 Eleventh Avenue South, Suite 248
Minneapolis, MN 55415
auca.org

Architectural Engineering Institute
1801 Alexander Bell Drive, First Floor
Reston, VA 20191-4400
aeinstitute.org

Associated General Contractors of America (AGC)
1957 E Street NW
Washington, DC 20006
agc.org

Association for Engineering Geologists
Department of Geology and Geophysics
Texas A&M University
TAMU 3115
College Station, TX 77843-3115
aegweb.org

National Association of Women in Construction (NAWIC)
327 South Adams Street
Fort Worth, TX 76104
nawic.org

CHAPTER

8

ELECTRICAL AND ELECTRONICS ENGINEERING

The largest of all engineering disciplines, with over 225,000 engineers, is the field of electrical and electronics engineering. It seems to be the single area most in touch with today's world. From Game Boys to remote navigational systems for unmanned spy planes, the work of electrical and electronics engineers is the result of both electrical phenomena and technology. Electrical and electronics engineers have significantly changed modern-day life and brought high technology into our homes and workplaces.

According to the *Occupational Outlook Handbook*, electrical and electronics engineers "design, develop, test, and supervise the manufacture of electrical and electronic equipment. Some of this equipment includes power generation, controlling, and transmission devices used by electric utilities; and electric motors, machinery controls, lighting, and wiring in buildings, automobiles, aircraft, radar and navigation systems, and broadcast and communications systems. Many electrical and electronics engineers also work in areas closely related to computers. However, engineers whose work is related exclusively to computer hardware are considered computer hardware engineers."

THE NATURE OF THE WORK

There are numerous subclassifications of electrical engineering that encompass virtually every facet of our lives. Little, if anything, we take for granted in our daily existence would have been possible without the intervention of skilled electrical engineers. In fact, the classifications and categories rapidly blur in today's technology. It is very difficult to distinguish where an electronics engineer's contributions end and a specialist engineer's begin in control systems, yet both professionals are electrical engineers. In fact, the term *electrical engineering* is really very limiting, as there are more than thirty classifications under the umbrella of electrical engineering. However, there are four well-recognized branches of electrical engineering—power, communications, electronics, and control systems. These branches and their subcategories are shown in Figure 8.1.

Power

Electrical engineers who specialize or concentrate in the power field are involved in power generation, transmission, distribution, application, or in combinations of these branches.

Power Generation

Power generation is merely converting energy from a static form to one that is adaptable to our needs. This means that engineers working in this field design systems that can utilize static forms of energy (water power, solar power, fossil fuels, and chemical agents) to produce usable electric power.

Ideally, engineers strive for the maximum in efficiency; however, there is no such thing as totally efficient power. Determining how this energy is to be converted is the responsibility of power generation engineers. These are specially trained electrical engineers who design the best methods of conversion of one form of energy (static) to the desired form of energy— electrical power. Because there are different sources of power, the techniques electrical engineers devise to generate power vary.

Water power is harnessed through the use of hydraulics. It is used to turn electric generators called turbines, which use the water's motion to spin the turbine blades and drive the generators. The end result is electric power.

*Fossil fuels—oil, gas, and coal—*are known as "nonrenewable resources" with particular problems of their own. Besides the problem of a potentially uncontrolled demand on an inherently limited supply, there is the overriding problem of environmental pollution that is produced when fossil fuels are converted into electrical power. Specialized electrical engineers

Figure 8.1

Branches of Electrical and Electronics Engineering

Power engineers are involved in:

Power generation from

Water power

Fossil fuels (oil, gas, and coal)

Geothermal energy

Solar energy

Nuclear energy

Transmission and distribution of power

Applications of power

Communications engineers are involved with:

Equipment or apparatus

Transmission

Switching and circuits

Systems

Traffic

Commercial applications

Plant engineering

Acoustical engineering

Electronics engineers are involved with electronic equipment for:

Computer hardware

Telecommunication systems

Radio

Television

Consumer products

Navigational systems

Biomedical applications

Control systems engineers are involved in:

Automatic regulators

Numerical control of machines

Computer control of industrial processes

Robotics

deal with both aspects of the problem: how to best utilize a limited resource to produce power and how to generate this power with the least amount of environmental damage (pollution). These design criteria apply from the design stages to the final operation of the power plant.

Geothermal, solar, and nuclear power generation offer some of the greatest challenges to electrical engineers. These power sources are considered almost limitless. However, harnessing and converting them to usable power that is both efficient and safe can be quite challenging. Therefore, the training of electrical engineers who work in these areas is highly specialized.

Geothermal energy conversion, or the generation of electrical power from natural sources of heat deep within the earth's crust, is experimental. Electrical engineers have coupled the conventional form of steam-driven, turbine-powered generation with some radically new technology, enabling them to convert the earth's core heat into a reliable and controlled source of steam power. This power will drive tomorrow's electrical generation plants. Though nonrenewable, geothermal energy can probably, according to the experts, be considered limitless, as a fairly large percentage of thermal energy is returned to its source.

Solar power generation, although used extensively in our space program, has yet to achieve a cost-effective place in power-generation schemes. Converting energy from the sun to usable quantities of electric power is still considered to be in the experimental stages. Therefore, the future holds great promise for solar energy, and electrical engineers who specialized in power generation are working on more cost-effective methods of converting our limitless supplies of sunlight and heat from geothermal sources to electricity to meet our future needs.

Nuclear power, once thought to be the answer to our power requirements, produces many problems for electrical engineers. While nuclear power is efficient, it has inherent dangers. Under carefully controlled applications, engineers have incorporated both efficiency and safety into the design and operation of nuclear power plants, which convert nuclear energy into heat that turns water into steam to drive turbines and produce electricity.

Compared to other forms of power generation, nuclear power is clean and relatively pollutant free. However, the way the power is produced creates very unique and challenging problems for electrical engineers. Security—the physical containment of the nuclear power source—is of utmost importance. There must be stringent monitoring of the source and means of ensuring that the potentially hazardous energy is kept in its place, under control. Special techniques and controls must be developed to prevent and guard against leaks and equipment failures.

In addition, the electrical engineers designing nuclear projects must take into account and plan for acceptable means of disposing of waste generated by nuclear power production. This area of power generation requires the expertise of several electrical engineering classifications.

Transmission and Distribution

While electrical engineers devise efficient ways of producing power, others work at maximizing the transmission and distribution of electricity by more efficient methods.

The transmission and distribution of electrical power is governed by the strict rules of physics. There are power losses no matter how well a distribution and transmission network is designed. In order to minimize these losses and provide the maximum power transfer, electrical engineers design and implement schemes that utilize power transformers to convert raw electrical power to a high voltage for more effective transfer over long distances with less loss.

Applications

As power reaches its desired location, other electrical engineers have already been at work developing effective methods of using the power. These engineers specialize in power applications that can range from the design of lighting systems for major cities to schemes for the electrical motors driving some of the very latest rapid mass transportation systems.

These engineers must juggle several problems at the same time. They must be conscious of the overall cost impact that technological developments will have on the end product and, at the same time, be energy conservationists, squeezing every last possible watt of energy out of a power source. These same engineers also develop the machines that manufacture the products that make our lifestyle what it is. As such, they work in automotive engineering and paper and steel manufacturing as well as a host of other large and small consumer-related businesses.

Communications

Electrical engineers who specialize or concentrate in the communications field are involved in equipment engineering, transmission engineering, switching and circuits, systems engineering, traffic engineering, commercial applications engineering, plant engineering, or acoustical engineering. Communications engineering has a direct impact on the production or operation of almost everything that touches our lives.

Electrical engineers in this branch design systems that receive, transmit, and deliver information in audio as well as video form. The radio, television, and telephone are all the products of electrical engineers specializing in communications. Recent technological advances, especially the joining of computer technology with information processing and distribution, have provided opportunities that were only dreams to communications engineers. These engineers have made major contributions to military and civilian air traffic control, communications technology, and instrumentation used in space. The highly sophisticated surveillance receivers used in electronic warfare systems are yet another example of the type of work in the communications branch of electrical and electronics engineering. There are several kinds of electrical engineers directly involved in the communications process.

Equipment Engineers

Equipment or apparatus engineers are electrical engineers involved in the design and implementation of devices that take information and translate or convert it into a form suitable for transmission to distant locations. In essence, electrical engineers build the radio and TV transmitters and receivers that provide society with communications, whatever the form. These forms of communication include the fax machine, the telephone, and computer-assisted technology that not only processes information but transmits it to a distant location where it can be used by others. These linkups also extend into space. Today, satellites serve as both transmitters and receivers, making worldwide transmission of data and images possible. Satellites act as relay centers high above the earth, linking distant points as if they were next door.

Transmission Engineers

Transmission engineers work with systems that include optical fiber, paired cable, and analog and/or digital equipment. They provide the pathways or channels for communications signals to be amplified and made reliable for such things as data and voice communications, including computer-to-computer data communications. It is very important for transmission engineers to thoroughly understand the science of wave propagation—the effect the earth and the atmosphere will have on a radio signal. In their work, transmission engineers design, develop, manufacture, market, and service products such as Internet hardware, navigational systems for ships, and high-frequency radios that require sophisticated methods of transmitting various types of information.

Switching and Circuit Engineers

These engineers specialize in switching circuitry. They are the control, direction, and "glue" for the entire communications effort. In addition, these engineers design and develop major switching centers in large cities and in the tiniest of computers embedded in medical devices. These switching centers are constantly monitoring the use and quality of communications traffic and transmission. If they sense an error they reroute the communications with hardly a flicker or lost bit of information.

Switching and circuit engineers' tools include circuits, components, batteries, exotic power supplies, and banks of computers with programmed responses to rapidly changing conditions. For example, the impact of semiconductor and computer technologies on the telecommunications industry resulted in the conversion from analog to digital integrated information systems. This meant that engineers needed to have strong knowledge of computer programming and systems analysis to program minicomputer-controlled systems for equipment used in industries as diverse as telecommunications and health.

Systems Engineers

Systems engineers specialize in improving the overall performance of switching systems. In general, they are among the most customer-oriented engineers in this field. They improve customer service by introducing new features and reducing communications costs. According to Frank Hecker in *What Systems Engineers Do* (available at hecker.org/writings/se.html), "Systems engineers apply their technical expertise in support of the sale of complex technological products, typically computer hardware, software, and/or services." Hecker outlines the major activities in which systems engineers engage. They include:

- Soliciting technical requirements from customers
- Giving presentations on and demonstrations of products

- Providing informal advice on what products might fulfill the customer's needs
- Writing more formal documents such as proposals and targeted white papers
- Serving as a point of contact for nonroutine technical issues at major accounts
- Assisting salespeople with the creation and execution of an overall sales strategy for an account

In *What Is Systems Engineering? A Consensus of Senior Systems Engineers* (available at sie.arizona.edu/sysengr/whatis/whatis.html), Terry Bahill and Frank Dean describe systems engineering as "an interdisciplinary process that ensures that the customer's needs are satisfied throughout a system's entire life cycle." Bahill and Dean state that systems engineers follow seven tasks:

1. Stating the problem
2. Investigating alternatives
3. Modeling the system
4. Integrating system elements together so they work as a whole
5. Launching the system (This means that they run the system to make sure that it does what it was intended to do.)
6. Assessing performance
7. Reevaluating the system

Traffic Engineers

The traffic engineer, yet another member of the communications team, is the direct link between a communications system and its users. While the title "traffic engineer" might seem to refer to the movement of vehicles on the highway, here it refers to those engineers concerned with the availability of adequate communications services to handle not only normal flow of voice and data through a system but overloads as well. Having said that, it is important to point out that some of these engineers are, in fact, concerned with the flow of vehicle traffic on streets and highways. They control this flow through the use of traffic light systems and electronic sensors.

Traffic engineers use a combination of engineering, planning, and accounting to perform their jobs. They study equipment capabilities and how to plot these capabilities against customer patterns of use. They study circuit operating efficiencies as well. Thus they ensure that a system can handle any demand without having excessive or unnecessary idle circuit time. They can be considered the "auditors" of the communications engineering field, assuring that all systems work as planned.

Commercial Engineers

Commercial engineers specialize in the service aspects of communications. This means that they study the public's needs for power and communications systems, especially the public's reaction to the actual services, the costs of those services, and any limitations that are of concern. These engineers are responsible for balancing rates (what a service costs the communications supplier) with revenues (how much the supplier can charge the user of this service). While some commercial engineers work for industry, many work for government regulatory agencies, where their knowledge of electrical and electronics engineering is valuable in setting and regulating government policy.

Plant Engineers

Plant engineers design all electrical and electronic aspects of a manufacturing facility. The work can include the design of generating plants, substations, and power distribution systems, but it also includes the design of state-of-the-art drive systems, digital regulators, motion controllers, programmable controllers, and microprocessors. Some plant engineers are responsible for designing the plant's computer system. Others are concerned with planning for the expansion of existing power and/or communications facilities and systems.

The plant engineer develops detailed studies that define the type and size of equipment required by the plant. They also oversee the selection and purchase of electrical equipment and supervise and support engineers from consulting firms that may be hired to design needed equipment. Plant engineers are responsible for starting up new equipment at the manufacturing facility.

Plant engineers also perform duties that are not usually associated with electrical or communications engineering. These duties include general day-to-day building operations and negotiating with local communities to secure land and rights of way.

Acoustical Engineers

Acoustical engineers specialize in the design and implementation of devices that convert sound to a form suitable for transmission over radio waves and then reproduce it through loudspeakers. They are concerned with the design of sound studios, concert halls, and other public facilities where people go to hear and see movies, concerts, and other forms of entertainment.

Acoustical engineers are also concerned with sound levels and noise pollution. Without them, what might be music to one person could be a source of pain to others. They constantly monitor the levels of sounds and formulate charts identifying what is a safe sound and when a sound becomes hazardous to people. Many of these engineers are also employed in industry to help ensure that workers are not subjected to dangerous noise levels in offices and industrial sites.

Electronics

Of the four well-recognized classifications of electrical engineering, perhaps electronics has the distinction of being the most visible and, therefore, the most "glamorous." There are many subcategories of electronics engineering, ranging from the mix of electronics and physiology (biomedical or clinical engineering) to computers and data processing. Along with these fields there are literally dozens of fields that affect our lives and our futures, such as consumer and home electronics, including digital televisions, radios, DVDs, CDs, and VCRs.

Electronics engineers can be involved in many areas of this industry including research and development; the investigation of new components and devices; the design of circuits, components, equipment, and computer programs; and the production of all types of electronic devices. In addition, these engineers advise on materials required and the cost of production of specific components or devices.

The shrinking of computer systems from room-sized machines to handheld devices has opened new, challenging opportunities for electronics engineers. The development and enhancement of electronic aids in air, land, and sea navigation have made travel increasingly safe and opened many new opportunities for electronics engineers. Likewise, medical electronics offers expanding opportunities for electronics engineers. Bionic replacements for body parts, artificial hearts, pacemakers (electronic regulators for failing hearts), and devices based on sonar are just some of the examples of biomedical advancements that are contributing to this growth area.

Control Systems

The control systems specialty deals with the analysis and design of automatic regulators, guidance systems, numerical control of machines, computer control of industrial processes, and robotics. Electrical engineers in this area are concerned with the identification of system stability, system performance criteria, and optimization.

Control systems are essential in the automation of complex manufacturing processes used in making products such as gasoline, detergent, appliances, food and medicine, and household items that are used every day. Control systems engineers design the devices that manufacture cars, cut out patterns in sheet metal, assemble parts, move objects, and control our environment.

Today, most home appliances have sophisticated control systems. Precision required in the manufacture of many electrical, electronic, and mechanical products is made possible by the control systems engineer. Together with other electronics engineers, they also produce machines to make other machines—or robots.

Related Fields

Many individuals trained as electrical engineers apply their knowledge to related engineering fields. A few of the common related applications are described here.

Electromechanical

Probably the most common merger of electricity with another field occurs when mechanical design is required to activate some new electrical device. Operation of the machine may depend upon some intricate mechanical apparatus without which the innovative electrical design is useless.

Electrochemical

Opportunities for electrical engineers in the chemical and allied industries occur primarily in the power field.

The chemical composition of materials used in electrical applications may be critical in some applications. To ensure consistent results, the electrical engineer may have to delve deeply into the chemical composition of materials. For example, for many years the presence of minute impurities in lead plates for storage batteries led to erratic performance. It was only through careful study and experimentation that unwanted impurities were weeded out and performance improved.

Manufacturing/Industry

Many practicing engineers move from their chosen specialty in a major engineering field to more general application in industrial or manufacturing settings. With years of experience in an industry or in manufacturing, electrical engineers are apt to grow away from their electrical engineering field and move into the broader field of management, where their principal activities are in the management of a production organization.

Heating, Ventilation, Air-Conditioning, and Refrigeration

It may be surprising to learn that heating, ventilation, air-conditioning, and refrigeration can be considered branches of electrical engineering. Usually, they are associated with the mechanical field. Many electrical engineers have become interested in the electrical specialties involved in these disciplines and have gradually grown to embrace all phases of the subject. Actually, these are three fairly well-defined fields that are very closely related and that can be combined to excellent advantage.

Heating and ventilation increasingly involve electric appliances for regulation, controls, and circulation. Additionally, electrical engineers are interested in the possibility of solar heat installations and of storage of heat for equalizing winter and summer temperatures. The applications employ the same techniques as refrigeration. Hence the combination of refrigeration with heating, ventilation, and air-conditioning comes as a matter of course.

Technical Sales

Many organizations that produce electrical or electronic devices or components employ electrical engineers in technical sales because these engineers have the background to discuss related electrical problems with prospective customers. As a general rule, sales ability is relatively well rewarded, and most engineers who enter this field remain in it, even though the application of engineering in their work may be slight.

Another sales opportunity for electrical engineers is known as an applications engineer. These specialists combine engineering and sales. For example, the manufacturer of arc welding equipment may require a sales engineer who can size up the requirements of a prospective customer, design welding equipment adapted for the customer's plant operation, and place the order in such a way that the supplier will be able to supervise, test, and make corrections where necessary for customer satisfaction.

Public Regulation

Work in public regulation consists largely of valuations of electrical plants and telecommunication systems, depreciation studies, and determination of rates. Knowledge of power generation or telecommunications is important, along with a good understanding of government and political science.

THE SETTINGS IN WHICH ELECTRICAL AND ELECTRONICS ENGINEERS WORK

According to Stephen Kahne, in *Careers and the Engineer*, "The computer revolution has had a pervasive influence on all aspects of the electrical engineering field. One significant career branch includes all jobs for which the computer is the object of the job. The rest of the field of electrical engineering involves computers as an essential enabling technology—whether simply as a tool for communication or as the intelligent engine for performing design and control actions." This means that every setting in which electrical engineers work now involves extensive work with computers, whether the setting is industry, consulting, government, or teaching.

Industry

Almost every part of the industrialized world's economy employs electrical engineers. The following is a partial list of the industrial settings in which electrical engineers can be employed:

Aeronautical/aerospace
Automotive
Automation and robotics
Chemical and petrochemical

Computers

Communication and telecommunication systems

Construction

Controls

Defense

Electric utilities

Electronic and solid-state circuitry

Environmental

Food and beverage

Glass, ceramics, and metals

Instrumentation

Integrated circuits

Machine tools

Medical

Mining and metallurgy

Nuclear

Oceanography

Optoelectronics

Pulp and paper

Textiles

Transportation

Water and wastewater

Consulting

Although some electrical engineers join consulting firms upon graduation and generally work in computer programming and software applications, most engineers who become consultants usually have expertise in a specific engineering discipline and have practiced successfully in that field for many years. Experienced engineers in consulting organizations render complete services to their customers, including preliminary surveys, development, design, financing, operation, and management on large- or small-scale projects.

One phase of consulting engineering that has proved increasingly attractive is the development of specialty products. In this area, consultants start with the client's idea and work with the client in the research, design, testing, patent protection, manufacturing, and marketing for the product.

Other consulting electrical engineers specialize in appraisals or rates for utility industries and government agencies. Still others may serve as expert witnesses in public hearings or in litigation.

Government Service

Electrical engineers are employed at federal, state, and local levels. Some electrical engineers work in such areas as military or civilian air traffic control, communications technologies, space technologies, surveillance systems, and patent applications.

Electrical engineers in the federal service are employed by such agencies as the U.S. Department of Defense, U.S. Food and Drug Administration, NASA, the U.S. Patent Office, the Bureau of Standards, and numerous federal commissions. Electrical engineers in state and local government service may work for many different agencies, but in particular regulatory agencies such as commerce commission and transportation agencies.

Teaching

Many engineers go directly into teaching, usually at the college and university level, or turn to teaching after years of successful practice. The teaching profession is very rewarding because it provides the opportunity to influence a new generation of engineers.

Teaching usually affords engineers time for research, writing, and consulting. Not infrequently, research undertaken in an engineering school leads to worthwhile inventions. In recognition of this, some schools have set up foundations to reward research that develops ideas and products for the benefit of society.

EDUCATION AND OTHER QUALIFICATIONS

In addition to the basic science and math that all engineering students take, electrical engineering students take required courses in mathematical logic and set theory, algorithms, numerical methods and analysis, probability and statistics, and operating systems. They also take courses in computer science and programming techniques. Depending on the expertise of faculty members at a particular university, students then specialize in one of the branches or subdivisions of electrical engineering: power generation, control systems, communications, or electronics. Each of the professional societies in electrical engineering can provide a list of institutions offering academic programs beyond high school in electrical engineering fields.

OUTLOOK FOR THE FUTURE

As stated earlier, electrical and electronics engineering is a rapidly changing field. Consider Stephan Kahne's observation that only "a few decades ago, most [electrical engineers] worked in the power utility industry. Then came vacuum tube electronics. . . . Solid-state devices and systems [also] dominate[d]." Now fiber optics, microprocessors, and digital systems are among the newest technologies driving the future of the field.

Because of this explosive growth, the job outlook for electrical and electronics engineers continues to be very good. Currently, most employers of electrical and electronics engineers cannot find enough good engineers to fill the demand. With the phenomenal growth of electronics in every industry, but in particular in the biomedical industry, the demand for electrical and electronics engineers is expected to be very strong through 2008.

EARNINGS

The National Society of Professional Engineers (NSPE) reported that electrical engineers graduating with a bachelor's degree in 2000 received an average starting salary offer of $48,613, a 7.6 percent increase over 1999. In 2001, the National Association of Colleges and Employers reported that bachelor's graduates in electrical and electronics engineering received starting offers averaging $51,910. This represented another 6.7 percent increase and demonstrated that even in a tight job market, electrical and electronics engineers continued to command higher rates of pay.

For those completing graduate degrees in 2001, the earnings were even higher. Master's-degree candidates averaged $63,812, and Ph.D. candidates averaged $79,241.

Overall the median annual earnings of electrical engineers were $64,910 in 2000, with the lowest 10 percent earning less than $41,740 and the highest 10 percent earning more than $94,490. For electronics engineers who are not in the computer industry, the median annual earnings of electronics engineers were $64,830 during the same time period. The lowest 10 percent of electronics engineers earned less than $43,070, and the highest 10 percent earned more than $94,330.

ADDITIONAL SOURCES OF INFORMATION

Acoustical Society of America (ASA)
500 Sunnyside Boulevard
Woodbury, NY 11797
http://asa.aip.org/index.html

American Electronics Association (AEA)
5201 Great American Parkway, Suite 520
P.O. Box 54990
Santa Clara, CA 95054
aeanet.org

American Public Power Association (APPA)
2301 M Street NW
Washington, DC 20037
appanet.org

American Society of Heating, Refrigerating and Air-Conditioning
    Engineers (ASHRAE)
1791 Tullie Circle NE
Atlanta, GA 30329
ashrae.org

Armed Forces Communications and Electronics Association (AFCEA)
4400 Fair Lakes Court
Fairfax, VA 22033
afcea.com

Association for Computing Machinery
1515 Broadway
New York, NY 10036
acm.org

Association for Electric Motors, Their Control and Application (SMMA)
P.O. Box 378
Sherborn, MA 01770-0378
smma.org

Association for Facilities Engineers (AFE)
Formerly the American Institute of Plant Engineers (AIPE)
8180 Corporate Park Drive, Suite 305
Cincinnati, OH 45242
afe.org

Association of Energy Engineers (AEE)
4025 Pleasantdale Road, Suite 420
Atlanta, GA 30340
aeecenter.org

Association of Energy Services Professionals (AESP)
7491 North Federal Highway, #c5, Suite 261
Boca Raton, FL 33487
aesp.org

Audio Engineering Society, Inc. (AES)
60 East Forty-Second Street, Room 2520
New York, NY 10165
aes.org

Electric Power Research Institute (EPRI)
3412 Hillview Avenue
Palo Alto, CA 94303
epri.com

Electric Power Supply Association (EPSA)
1401 H Street NW, Suite 760
Washington, DC 20005
EPSA.org

Fiber Optic Association (FOA)
Fotec, Inc.
151 Mystic Avenue
Medford, MA 02155
std.com/fotec

IEEE Communications Society
305 East Forty-Seventh Street
New York, NY 10017-2303
comsoc.or

IEEE Computer Society Offices
1730 Massachusetts Avenue NW
Washington, DC 20036-1992
computer.org/contact.htm

Illuminating Engineering Society of North America (IESNA)
120 Wall Street, Seventeenth Floor
New York, NY 10005-4001
iesna.org

Institute for Interconnecting and Packaging Electronic Circuits (IPC)
2215 Sanders Road
Northbrook, IL 60062
ipc.org

Institute of Electrical and Electronics Engineers, Inc. (IEEE)
Three Park Avenue, Seventeenth Floor
New York, NY 10016-5997
ieee.org

IEEE Society Offices:
IEEE Communications Society (see separate listing)
IEEE Components Packaging, and Manufacturing Technology Society
IEEE Computer Society (see separate listing)
IEEE Electron Devices Society
IEEE Engineering in Medicine and Biology Society
IEEE Lasers and Electro-Optics Society
IEEE Power Engineering Society
IEEE Signal Processing Society
IEEE Solid-State Circuits Society

Instrumentation, Systems and Automation Society (ISA)
P.O. Box 12277
67 Alexander Drive
Research Triangle Park, NC 27709
isa.org

International Association of Lighting Designers (IALD)
The Merchandise Mart
200 World Trade Center, Suite 487
Chicago, IL 60654
iald.org

International Municipal Signal Association (IMSA)
165 East Union Street
Newark, NY 14513
imsasafety.org

National Association of Electrical Distributors (NAED)
1100 Corporate Square Drive, Suite 100
St. Louis, MO 63132
naed.org

National Association of Power Engineers, Inc.
1 Springfield Street
Chicopee, MA 01013
powerengineers.com

National Council of Acoustical Consultants (NCAC)
66 Morris Avenue, Suite 1A
Springfield, NJ 07081-1409
ncac.com/index.html

National Electrical Manufacturers Association (NEMA)
1300 North Seventeenth Street, Suite 1847
Rosslyn, VA 22209
nema.org

National Electrical Manufacturers Representatives Association
    (NEMRA)
200 Business Park Drive, Suite 301
Armonk, NY 10504
nemra.org

Optical Society of America (OSA)
2010 Massachusetts Avenue NW
Washington, DC 20036
osa.org

Power Transmission Distributors Association (PTDA)
6400 Shafer Court, Suite 670
Rosemont, IL 60018-4909
ptda.org

Refrigeration Service Engineers Society (RSES)
1666 Rand Road
Des Plaines, IL 60016-3552
rses.org

Robotic Industries Association (RIA)
900 Victors Way
P.O. Box 3724
Ann Arbor, MI 48106
robotics.org

Society of Manufacturing Engineers (SME)
One SME Drive
P.O. Box 930
Dearborn, MI 48121-0930
sme.org

Society of Motion Picture and Television Engineers (SMPTE)
595 West Hartsdale Avenue
White Plains, NY 10607
smpte.org

SPIE—International Society for Optical Engineering
P.O. Box 10
Bellingham, WA 98227-0010
spie.org

C H A P T E R

INDUSTRIAL ENGINEERING

According to the Institute of Industrial Engineers, "Industrial engineers figure out how to do things better." They apply their knowledge to a wide range of issues and in a broad array of settings. That is why industrial engineering is considered one of the top four engineering disciplines. In fact, industrial engineers are critical to the overall strategic planning of corporations, nonprofit organizations, and government agencies and often serve as the link between engineering and management.

Industrial engineers have always used their expertise to improve quality and productivity. In the past, this may have meant conducting worker time studies or designing a new facility layout. Today, industrial engineers use a "systems" approach to solving problems. An overall systems approach means that industrial engineers no longer study only one segment of the business. Instead, they look at the entire process as a continuous flow of goods and information, and their primary responsibility is to improve that flow.

THE NATURE OF THE WORK

Industrial engineers use their basic knowledge of engineering, organizational behavior, and the sciences to design, plan, and control production and service systems. They tend to take the "big picture" approach and use automation, computer-integrated systems, computer science, computer engineering, and information technology as tools to improve productivity, quality, and efficiency. They plan, organize, and carry out projects in a wide variety of settings. Because industrial engineers typically enjoy human interaction, they balance the needs and abilities of people with the availability and characteristics of materials and energy, as well as equipment and facilities. They seek the best alternatives to bridge the gap between management and operations. With this broad focus, industrial engineering has many facets.

According to the Institute for Industrial Engineering, industrial engineers become involved with such things as advancing manufacturing methods utilizing robotics; computer and information systems; energy management; engineering economy (financial engineering); facilities planning and design, including materials handling; human factors or ergonomics; human resources management; operations research and computer simulation; organization and job design; production and inventory control; and quality assurance; as well as warehousing and distribution work measurement.

Industrial engineers get involved with such things as:

- Long-range planning and facilities design for a major transportation facility
- Robotics programs at a major automotive manufacturer
- Assisting in the design and installation of operations systems for semiconductor facilities
- Creating more productive work flow within a hospital or other health institution
- Designing a computer-based management information system for a financial institution

Industrial engineers are concerned with performance measures and standards, research of new products and product applications, methods to improve use of scarce resources, and many other challenges. Industrial engineers relate to the total picture of productivity improvement where productivity means getting the most out of a system for the least input.

Industrial engineers also look at the right combination of human resources, natural resources, and man-made structures and equipment to optimize productivity. They address the issue of motivating people as well as determining what tools should be used and how they should be used.

Industrial engineers are involved in such areas as operations research, applied behavioral science, and systems engineering.

- *Operations research.* In this area, industrial engineers describe a situation in mathematical models to determine the best course of action to recommend to management.
- *Applied behavioral science.* This area combines engineering principles with behavioral sciences such as sociology, psychology, and anthropology to improve the management function. Industrial engineers study how organizations work and how they can work better. Their approach is scientific and quantitative. The management of technology has become a major application of this area.
- *Systems engineering.* Industrial engineers in this area are concerned with improving complex systems in manufacturing, transportation, housing, health-care delivery, energy allocation, environmental control, criminal justice, and education.

Logistics and Supply Chain Management

Expanding areas of opportunity in industrial engineering are logistics and supply chain management. *Logistics* is often defined as the management of inventory at rest and in motion. Industrial engineers who work in this area cut costs, improve service, and boost profitability by taking a systems approach to focus on getting goods and services to the marketplace in a timely, cost-effective manner.

Today companies are under constant pressure to reduce the inventory of supplies needed to make products and to decrease the number of products that are in their warehouses and have not been sold. Companies must also eliminate wasteful and unnecessary steps in getting their products or services to market. At the same time, more and more companies are selling their products and services around the world. This has created what are called global markets.

The creation of global markets means that many companies have a large number of locations, plants, warehouses, vendors, and customers. *Supply chain management* focuses on globalization and information management tools. It brings together the purchase of supplies, the overall operation of an organization, and the process of turning raw materials into products, and ultimately customer satisfaction.

Industrial engineers who work in the area of supply chain management add value to products or services, improve the quality of those products or services, reduce costs, and increase profits. These industrial engineers work closely with outside organizations that supply their employer with the resources needed to run the business. They are very involved with the field of E-commerce and are knowledgeable about the most current supply chain software.

Using technical expertise and strong communications skills, industrial engineers in supply chain management become involved in selecting suppliers to their organization, negotiating prices from suppliers, and evaluating overall performance of company operations, transportation systems, and inventory and warehousing. They may also analyze the practices of the companies or organizations with which they compete for business to assure that their employer is remaining competitive in the marketplace. This type of analysis is known as *benchmarking*.

The five key issues for logistics and supply chain management engineers are movement of product, movement of information, time/service, cost reduction, and integration or cooperation within the company, as well as between the company and its customers and between the company and its vendors. When new solutions are found, the results for the organization can be significant cost reductions, a new competitive edge, improved products or services, and increased profits. The results for the engineer are opportunities for advancement, particularly to upper management and executive positions.

Executive Management

It has been said that industrial engineering can be a "fast track" to executive management. That is because successful industrial engineers possess the ability to communicate effectively and to manage projects and multiple tasks. To further develop these skills and abilities, industry is increasingly offering programs to prepare industrial engineers for management positions. For example, Eaton Corporation is a global, diversified industrial manufacturer. It is considered to be a leader in fluid power systems; electrical power quality, distribution, and control; automotive engine air management and fuel economy; and intelligent truck systems for fuel economy and safety.

Eaton Corporation provides a unique Leadership Development Program (LDP) within its Fluid Power Group for new engineering graduates. The program is well suited to industrial engineers because it targets graduates who want to move into management and progress to positions of business leadership through a fast-track career development process.

The Eaton LDP is targeted to developing management skills through progressively challenging work experiences that establish technical expertise and provide cross-functional experiences and opportunities to develop leadership skills. It is a three-year experience with four to five different assignments. The assignments are selected to provide progressive work experiences, a variety of challenges, and significant career growth. The assignments are in the functional areas of engineering, operations, technical sales and marketing, and finance, and they include opportunities to gain experience in managing human resources.

Upon completion of the LDP, graduates have been exposed to Eaton's businesses and have worked in various functions and locations. In addition, they know Eaton's customers and understand their overall needs. Potential jobs at the end of the LDP can include leadership roles in such areas as operations, sales and marketing, and product line management.

THE SETTINGS IN WHICH INDUSTRIAL ENGINEERS WORK

Industrial engineers can pursue their careers in a wide variety of work settings. Industrial engineering is performed in all major manufacturing industries as classified by the federal government's Standard Industrial Classification (SIC) code. In addition to the manufacturing sector, industrial engineers are employed in such diverse areas as accounting, merchandising, banks, hospitals, government and social service agencies, transportation, and construction industries. Interestingly, the National Association of Colleges and Employers reports that the most aggressive new recruiter of industrial engineers is the electrical and electronics manufacturing sector.

The airline industry, hospitals, management consulting and logistical consulting firms, and companies such as IBM, Caterpillar, GE, Ford Motor

Company, General Motors, Eaton Corporation, Rockwell International, FedEx, and UPS are all major employers of industrial engineers.

EDUCATION AND OTHER QUALIFICATIONS

Mathematics and science play a key role in the industrial engineer's knowledge. At least four years of high school math, including calculus and trigonometry, plus three years of science, including chemistry and physics, are important preparation for an industrial engineering major in college.

The typical curriculum for a bachelor's degrees in industrial engineering is focused, disciplined, and structured and typically includes two years of basic mathematics and science (physics and chemistry); introductory engineering; the humanities, social sciences, and English; and two years of study in one of the following major areas of specialization in industrial engineering:

Engineering economics
Decision analysis
Human factors (interactions between humans and machines or
   computers)
Manufacturing systems
Optimization/logistics
Production, distribution, and material handling
Statistics
Stochastic systems

Industrial engineering is offered at approximately one hundred accredited universities in the United States and Canada. A list of these institutions can be obtained from the Institute of Industrial Engineers (iie.org).

In addition to a college degree, increasing numbers of employers, particularly international companies and consulting firms, are placing a great deal of value on industrial engineers who hold a professional engineering license. The professional engineering license (P.E.) documents mastery of the engineering field and qualifies the industrial engineer to work on international projects and to lead engineering and cross-functional teams.

The first step in the licensing process is passing the Engineering in Training (EIT) test. This is usually taken during the senior year of college.

The EIT exam is the same for all engineering disciplines, and it includes questions from basic industrial engineering courses such as engineering economics, production/operations, management and systems, and manufacturing processes and systems. More information on professional licensing is available from the National Society of Professional Engineers at nspe.org/lc-home.asp.

OUTLOOK FOR THE FUTURE

As more and more organizations seek to increase productivity and improve quality, the need for industrial engineers will grow. Every indicator points to an excellent outlook for future growth in the field of industrial engineering. Industrial engineers will be in great demand not merely because they are engineers but also because of how they apply their engineering skills.

The increased demand for industrial engineers is due in great part to the need for organizations to raise their level of productivity through careful, systematic approaches to production and to improve the quality of their goods and services. Even nonprofit organizations will increasingly use industrial engineers to sustain their position as useful service entities.

Because of the demand for industrial engineers, the profession is extremely attractive in terms of financial rewards. Business rewards those who make an organization more profitable, and the industrial engineer does exactly that. In fact, salaries for industrial engineers are among the highest for all engineering disciplines, and many industrial engineers move quickly into management, making the outlook for continued personal and professional growth excellent.

EARNINGS

According to *U.S. News and World Report*, industrial engineering is the third-highest-paying profession among major engineering degrees. In 2000, the median annual salary for industrial engineers was $58,580. That means that half of the industrial engineers earned more than $58,580 and half made less. The Bureau of Labor Statistics reports that the lowest 10 percent of industrial engineers earned less than $38,140, and the highest 10 percent earned more than $86,370. Median annual earnings in the manufacturing industries, the sector employing the largest numbers of industrial engineers, ranged from $58,000 in the aircraft industry to $63,000 in the automotive industry.

The National Association of Colleges and Employers' 2001 salary survey reported that bachelor's-degree graduates in industrial engineering received starting offers averaging about $48,320. Master's-degree graduates averaged $56,265 a year, and Ph.D. graduates averaged $59,800.

ADDITIONAL SOURCES OF INFORMATION

Institute of Industrial Engineers
25 Technology Park
Norcross, GA 30092
iienet.org

Society of Manufacturing Engineers
One SME Drive
P.O. Box 930
Dearborn, MI 48121-0930
sme.org

International Society of Logistics
8100 Professional Place, Suite 211
Hyattsville, MD 20785
sole.org

Intelligent Transportation Systems, America
400 Virginia Avenue SW, Suite 800
Washington, DC 20024-2730
itsa.org

CHAPTER

MATERIALS SCIENCE ENGINEERING

In the world of materials science engineering, big news is always small! That is because most materials science engineers work with the molecular structures of a wide variety of materials.

Where civil engineers design and build bridges that connect one side of a river to another, materials science engineers make sure that the molecular structure of the asphalt, the steel, and the concrete will withstand environmental conditions and the weight of the vehicles that will cross the bridge every day. They will specify and test the materials to make sure that they will not fail and endanger the lives of the motorists who use the bridge.

In addition to testing materials, materials science engineers work to make materials stronger, lighter, more durable, capable of withstanding high temperatures or low temperatures, and resistant to corrosion, stresses, and/or breakage. Many products are limited by the characteristics of the materials from which they are made. That is why materials science engineers work to create new materials. Their goal is to improve the performance of existing materials and products and to invent new materials and products that meet our changing needs.

An excellent example is the composite material that has replaced steel in many parts of today's automobiles. In addition to changing the design of cars, composite materials have had a positive impact on the environment because they have increased gas mileage. Likewise, the materials in snowboards and water skis have enhanced performance and enjoyment of these sports. In many ways, materials science engineers play a key role in developing new technologies and new products because they deal with the production of materials that have properties that solve problems and are suitable for practical use.

THE NATURE OF THE WORK

Materials science engineers are characterized by a high level of interest in physics and chemistry. They use their knowledge of these sciences to study the properties of various types of materials such as metals, ceramics, polymers (plastics), semiconductors, and combinations of materials called composites. The work of the materials science engineer is focused on the composition of materials: how materials are made and/or how materials behave under different conditions.

In order to do this work, materials science engineers use a wide range of high-tech instruments and techniques. A basic tool of the materials science engineer is the scanning electron microscope. This microscope uses a focused electron beam to scan the surface of a specimen. Signals are generated when the electrons and the specimen interact. These signals are analyzed to produce highly magnified images so that materials science engineers can deduce the chemical nature of the specimen.

In addition to the scanning electron microscope, materials science engineers also use scanning tunneling microscopes, atomic force microscopes, transmission electron microscopes, and analytical electron microscopes. All of these devices provide images of the most intricate details of the structure of materials so that the materials science engineer can better understand their properties and behaviors.

Materials science engineers use numerous technologically advanced techniques to study materials. Some of these techniques include rapid freezing or low gravity of space. In addition, they use high-speed computers to model the behavior of atoms, materials, components, and systems. These computers make it possible for some materials science engineers to create new materials without ever having to leave their desks!

Materials science engineers can be broken into four primary groups, depending on the materials with which they work. There are:

- Metallurgical engineers
- Ceramics engineers
- Plastics or polymers engineers
- Materials science engineers

Metallurgical Engineers

Metallurgical engineers work in mineral- and metal-related industries with various combinations of metals. This is a very broad field. It encompasses minerals, metals, and materials processing and manufacturing. There are five types of metallurgical engineering: mineral processing engineering, extractive metallurgy, process metallurgy, physical metallurgy, and welding engineering.

Mineral Processing Engineering

Mineral processing engineering takes into account the differences in physical and/or chemical properties of minerals to develop, manage, and control the processes for separating and concentrating minerals in associated waste rock.

Extractive Metallurgy

Extractive metallurgy is the removal of metals from ores, concentrates, and scrap. Engineers working in this area use water chemistry, electrochemistry, and/or thermal chemistry technologies to extract metal from its sources.

Process Metallurgy

Process metallurgy is the development and improvement of processes that make metals and alloys into useful products. These processes include alloying, forging, rolling, casting, and powdering.

Physical Metallurgy

Physical metallurgy is the study of the nature, structure, and physical properties of metals and their alloys in order to control various chemical, physical, and mechanical properties of the metals and alloys.

Welding Engineering

Welding engineering is concerned with joining materials together, particularly metals, to produce efficient joints while ensuring minimum damage to the integrity of the materials being joined.

Ceramics Engineers

Ceramics engineers work with nonmetallic, inorganic materials produced from raw materials that are, for the most part, abundant and relatively inexpensive. They may also work with materials that are chemically synthesized and not available in a natural state. Ceramic materials are used for a variety of purposes. The space program is a large consumer of ceramics. The heat shield tiles on the space shuttle, as well as space capsules and even missile nose cones, are made of specially formulated ceramic materials. Closer to home, the cements and bricks used in the construction of houses are also ceramic.

Ceramics engineers work with materials having a wide range of characteristics that can be exploited in the development of new products. For example, ceramic materials that are insulating yet magnetic make the household microwave oven possible. Replacements for human bones and teeth that are durable, lightweight, and strong are also made possible by ceramics engineering.

Ceramics engineers have also produced new applications for existing products such as glass. Glass fibers are now replacing metal wires in communications systems. Telephone companies can transmit voices and data using laser technology and optical glass fibers. A major advantage is that more information can be sent through a relatively smaller cable.

Additionally, fiber optics—as the application of glass fibers in communications is known—offers virtually no interference and less resistance than is commonly associated with conventional metal cables. For this reason, many existing telephone lines are being replaced with cables made of glass fibers. This technological advance would not have been possible without the efforts of the ceramics engineer.

Two segments of the electronics industry, electrical utility companies and semiconductor manufacturers, also rely heavily on the skills of the ceramics engineer. Electric utilities require huge ceramic insulators for their high-voltage power transmission lines. They also use smaller insulators on the poles in front of your house or apartment. These insulators protect workers and the public from stray electrical voltages and also prevent the loss of electricity to the ground.

The semiconductor industry could not exist without ceramics engineering. Ceramics are used as insulators and building blocks for the integrated circuits, or chips, that have made so many of today's products possible and affordable. These chips are used in calculators, watches, stereos, televisions, and communications satellites. There are other uses and applications for integrated circuits and semiconductors, but it would be safe to say that without the ceramics engineer's contributions, we wouldn't have the standard of living or the electrical and electronic aids we take for granted.

Other electronic components also rely on ceramics engineering. These include capacitors, resistors, and modern sensors that convert information to electrical impulses for further processing and are used in control systems as well as in medical electronics technology.

Plastics Engineers

Plastics engineers are engaged in the development, conversion, and applications of plastics. The plastics industry is one of the largest manufacturing industries in the United States and plays an important role in markets ranging from packaging and construction to transportation; consumer and institutional products; furniture and furnishings; electrical/electronic components; adhesives; inks and coatings; and others.

Plastic materials are produced by combining chains of hydrocarbon molecules known as polymers. How the hydrogen is combined with the carbon and how these chains are strung together are challenges for plastics engineers. For example, some plastics engineers design and manufacture such things as thermoplastic compounds and specialty compounds for specific uses. Some make custom-molded plastics needed to package products for a wide variety of industries. Still others conduct research on and test plastics technologies and processes. The research, analysis, modeling, design, and testing of new plastics generally involves such activities as compounding, extrusion, molding, working with nanoscale structures, biopolymer engineering, and multiscale modeling.

New plastics have replaced more traditional materials, such as metal, glass, and wood, in a wide variety of applications, such as in automobiles, computers, furniture, and packaging. Engineered plastics have revolutionized the world of materials, and plastics engineers are at the forefront of this development.

Materials Science Engineers

Materials science engineering combines several principles of physical metallurgy, ceramics, and polymer chemistry to develop the best materials for a particular use or application. The materials science engineer integrates most, if not all, of the techniques of materials science engineering to produce new materials or to make existing materials more useful as the needs of society and industry change. They study the properties and uses of metals, ceramics, polymers, and engineered composite materials. Composites, as the name implies, are combinations of materials. Often, thin fibers of metals or nonmetals are literally woven into a fabric. This fabric is placed in a mold and covered with an engineered plastic resin. The result is a lightweight, strong, and durable material that combines properties of the base materials with corrosion resistance and flexibility. Often, these engineered materials are clearly superior to the separate materials that compose them.

The aircraft industry, the space program, and even the auto industry are making increased use of these engineered materials. The stealth technology by which an object is made invisible to radar, for example, would not be possible without composite technology. In this application, materials are deliberately selected that will absorb rather than reflect radar waves, rendering the object mostly invisible to the radar operator.

In other, nonmilitary applications, substituting composite materials for more conventional metals or alloys has allowed commercial jet aircraft to fly farther and faster, with less fuel, than the noncomposite aircraft of just a few years ago.

Automobile manufacturers are major users of composites. The composite materials are used to replace metals that are heavier, not corrosion-resistant, or not as strong. Lightening an automobile's weight by using these lighter composites increases its fuel efficiency while ensuring corrosion resistance and strength.

Boats, campers, and trailers are made of fiberglass, a composite material that is much more useful and durable than the traditional wood or metal products it replaced. Fiberglass is a good example of composite engineering brought to the consumer level.

Nanotechnology

Nanotechnology is a new focus of many materials science engineers. Nanotechnology is the study and manufacture of structures and devices with dimensions about the size of a molecule. In fact, nanoparticles are only about a billionth of a meter in size—a nanometer. When these nanoparticles are clumped together, they usually have different qualities than materials made from larger particles. This is why nanotechnology has such great potential for the future and why the federal government has increased funding for nanotechnology research through the National Nanotechnology Initiative. Therefore, more advances in this area of materials science engineering are expected.

According to Eric Drexler in "Machine-Phase Nanotechnology" in the September 2001 issue of *Scientific American*, technology has continued to shrink microelectronics so that we are now on the threshold of being able to make devices on the molecular scale. This ability will drastically change manufacturing and greatly improve the properties of materials and the performance of devices. For example, Drexler believes that nanotechnology has the potential to have major impact on such important aspects of our lives as global warming and advanced medical technology. Specifically, nanotechnology has the potential to remove excess greenhouse gases from the atmosphere or to repair tissue such as skin or bone.

The *Chicago Tribune* identified other potential uses for nanomaterials in an article entitled "Small Specks Hold Big Potential" on April 23, 2001. They included "transistors, microscope tips, hydrogen containers, electron guns, and protective coatings for tools." In the health-care area, the delivery of medication is another area where nanometer-scale packages can control where the medicine is released in the body. By so doing, high-powered medication only goes to those parts of the body that need it.

While most of these possibilities seem very futuristic, it is important to note that nanotechnology has been around for a long time. It has only been recently that the full potential of nanomaterials has been recognized.

Therefore, it is expected that nanotechnology will create many new jobs and new industries for materials science engineers during the twenty-first century.

Job Functions of Materials Science Engineers

Whether materials science engineers specialize in metals, ceramics, polymers (plastics), semiconductors, electronic materials, or nanotechnology, they work in many different job functions. Some of these job functions are research, manufacturing, applications, technical sales, services, consulting, management, and writing and teaching.

Research

Working with the building blocks of matter, engineers can unlock the secrets of nature. Basic knowledge is discovered that can benefit people everywhere.

Manufacturing

This field deals with the production of high-quality, reliable, uniform, predictable materials. The materials science engineer is a vital contributor to this effort.

Applications

Applications engineers develop new ways, new processes, and new materials to make virtually any product. The materials science engineer helps a company by applying technology to improve existing products or to produce new, better ones.

Technical Sales

The engineer's skills in matching materials to products and products to applications combined with his or her communications skills make for the best of all possible sales representation. Thus, a materials science engineer can succeed where others might fail in the sale and marketing of products.

Services

Materials science engineers apply their problem-solving techniques and communications skills to help customers solve problems they have with products the engineer may have developed.

Consulting

Independent materials science engineers serve a variety of clients who have diverse needs. Many companies require the skills that only a materials science engineer possesses. When they do not employ materials science engineers, these companies must hire independent consultants. The consultant frequently provides the competitive and technological edge the company requires in order to grow and/or to expand markets.

Management

Engineers use a systematic approach to problem solving. For this reason, many serve as managers and supervisors, using their investigative skills to identify and solve a broad variety of problems, including the allocation of both material and human resources.

Writing and Teaching

Writing and teaching both build on communications skills and a desire to impart information. Materials science engineers can promote technology and train tomorrow's problem-solvers by teaching or publishing about their field and experiences. The ability to take a complex process, solution, or technology and explain it so that students can benefit is the mark of a true engineering professional.

THE SETTINGS IN WHICH MATERIALS SCIENCE ENGINEERS WORK

In today's economy, materials science engineers face the challenge of meeting current needs and developing new technologies in such diverse areas as medicine, food, energy, conservation, and pollution. Materials science engineers head many problem-solving teams charged with engineering new materials that will replace older, nonrenewable resources and improve our quality of life. In order to accomplish these tasks, they will be employed in the following areas:

- *Materials-producing companies.* These produce better materials more efficiently and cleanly and provide the raw ingredients to make the advanced machinery and equipment needed to solve other technological problems.

- *Manufacturing companies.* These utilize the services of the materials science engineer to more effectively manufacture products such as cars, appliances, electronics, aerospace equipment, other machinery, and medicine. The materials science engineer plays a vital role in improving materials, processes, product reliability and safety, chemical processing, paper, plastics, and textiles. In 2000, there were approximately thirty thousand materials science engineers employed in the United States. Most were employed in the manufacturing sector.

- *Service companies.* All companies that serve the public's needs rely on materials science engineers to maintain safe, reliable service. Examples of such services include airlines, railroads, and utilities.

- *Consulting firms.* These provide companies, institutions, and the government with independent outside help identifying problems in materials processing and performance. They also provide guidance in developing practical, economical solutions to a variety of materials problems.

- *The government.* It is a consumer, promoter, and regulator of materials, products, and technology. It needs the materials science engineer or scientist to provide a flow of accurate information so that policy decisions can be based on facts, not political whims.

- *Research institutes.* These may work under contract to the government or private industry to probe materials, processes, and product development, ensuring that when tomorrow's products are needed, the technology will be in place to produce them.

- *Schools and universities.* These provide the materials science engineer with the opportunity to share knowledge and to train the engineers who will become the problem-solvers of tomorrow.

EDUCATION AND OTHER QUALIFICATIONS

Like all of the other engineering disciplines, preparation for undergraduate study of materials science engineering begins in junior high school with appropriate math and science courses. It is recommended that future materials science engineers study three years of high school science, including chemistry and physics, and four years of high school mathematics through trigonometry or calculus. It is also necessary to take at least three years of high school English.

College course work for a bachelor's degree in materials science engineering will vary depending on the institution and on the specialization. Specializations and concentrations at the undergraduate level include materials, metals, minerals, ceramics, polymers, and electronic materials. However, most programs will include two years of mathematics, science, and basic engineering and then two years establishing the structure, processing, and properties relationships for all specializations. Electives allow a student to develop a concentration in a particular specialization, and a sequence of two design courses in the senior year serves as a capstone experience for the bachelor's degree.

Many materials science engineers continue their studies beyond the bachelor's degree in order to gain more knowledge and expertise in one of the areas of specialization. They obtain master's and/or doctoral degrees. The master's degree usually can be earned within two years after the B.S. The doctoral degree usually involves six years of study.

Because much of materials science engineering occurs in the laboratory, advanced degrees are much in demand. According to the Engineering Manpower Commission in Washington, D.C., there were about the same number of materials science engineers earning bachelor's, master's, and Ph.D.s. Few other engineering disciplines show such an even balance between undergraduate and graduate education.

There are more than eighty colleges and universities that award degrees in materials science engineering, metallurgical engineering, and/or ceramics engineering. A list of programs that have been accredited by the Accreditation Board of Engineering and Technology (ABET) can be found at crc4mse.org/resources/colleges.html.

The materials science engineering degree is extremely versatile; therefore, depending on career goals, some materials science engineers pursue study in such professional areas as business administration, medicine, management, and law.

OUTLOOK FOR THE FUTURE

According to the U.S. Bureau of Labor Statistics, "More materials engineers will be needed to develop new materials for electronics and plastics products. However, many of the manufacturing industries in which materials engineers are concentrated—such as primary metals and stone, clay, and glass products—are expected to experience declines in employment, reducing employment opportunities."

Increasingly, companies are contracting out their materials engineering work. This means that more opportunities can be expected in services industries such as engineering consulting firms. It is expected that other opportunities will develop as a result of the need to replace engineers who leave the field. Finally, discoveries in the areas of nanotechnology, superconductors, and buckminsterfullerenes have the potential to create entirely new industries. These new industries will create more openings for materials science engineers.

EARNINGS

The National Association of Colleges and Employers' 2001 salary survey reported that materials science engineering graduates received starting offers averaging $49,936 a year.

For all other materials science engineers, the U.S. Bureau of Labor Statistics found that their median annual earnings were $59,100 in 2000, with the lowest 10 percent earning less than $37,680, and the highest 10 percent earning over $87,630.

ADDITIONAL SOURCES OF INFORMATION

Aluminum Association (AA)
900 Nineteenth Street NW, Suite 300
Washington, DC 20006
aluminum.org

American Ceramics Society (ACerS)
P.O. Box 6136
Westerville, OH 43086-6136
acers.org

American Concrete Institute (ACI)
P.O. Box 9094
Farmington Hills, MI 48333
aci-int.org

American Institute of Mining, Metallurgical and Petroleum Engineers
Three Park Avenue
New York, NY 10016
http://aimeny.org

American Society for Metals
9639 Kinsman Road
Materials Park, OH 44073-0002
asm-intl.org

American Society for Testing and Materials (ASTM)
100 Barr Harbor Drive
West Conshohocken, PA 19428-2959
astm.org

Concrete Reinforcing Steel Institute (CRSI)
933 North Plum Grove Road
Schaumburg, IL 60173-4758
crsi.org

Materials Research Society
506 Keystone Drive
Warrendale, PA 15086-7573
mrs.org

Minerals, Metals, and Materials Society
184 Thorn Hill Road
Warrendale, PA 15086
tms.org

National Mining Association
1130 Seventeenth Street NW
Washington, DC 20036-4677
nma.org

Precast/Prestressed Concrete Institute (PCI)
175 West Jackson Boulevard, Suite 1859
Chicago, IL 60604
pci.org

Society for Mining, Metallurgy, and Exploration
8307 Shaffer Parkway
Littleton, CO 80127-4102
smenet.org

Society for the Advancement of Material and Process Engineering
   (SAMPE)
1161 Parkview Drive
Covina, CA 91724-3748
et.byu.edu/org/sampe

Society for Mining, Metallurgy, and Exploration (SME)
8307 Shaffer Parkway
Littleton, CO 80127-4102
smenet.org
SME-affiliated organizations include:
The Minerals, Metals and Materials Society
The Society of Petroleum Engineers
The Iron and Steel Society

Society of Plastics Engineers (SPE)
14 Fairfield Drive
Brookfield, CT 06804-0403
4spe.org

Society of the Plastics Industry
1801 K Street NW, Suite 600
Washington, DC 20006
plasticsindustry.org

C H A P T E R

11

MECHANICAL ENGINEERING

Mechanical engineering is one of the most exciting engineering fields because it offers breadth, flexibility, and individuality. Mechanical engineering is an extremely creative profession. The work done by these engineers varies by function and industry. Some of the specialties that mechanical engineers pursue include applied mechanics; computer-aided design and manufacturing; energy systems; pressure vessels and piping; and heating, refrigeration, and air-conditioning systems.

In the manufacturing sector, mechanical engineers working in laboratory and field-testing may test products as diverse as high-performance race tires and artificial heart valves. Those specializing in computer-aided design, finite element analysis, or mechanics of composites will determine the proper performance characteristics of the product's materials. For example, in the design and manufacture of cell phones, it is important to determine that the phone will not break if dropped.

In general, mechanical engineers take a broad outlook when solving complex problems. Mechanical engineers work in such areas as power generation, energy conversion, machine design, manufacturing and automation, and control of engineering systems.

Mechanical engineers hold a unique position in the engineering field because they not only design, develop, and produce devices for consumers, they also design, develop, and produce many tools required by other engineers. Therefore, their role continually expands to keep pace with technology. Mechanical engineers will always be vital to the success of newly emerging technology fields such as nanotechnology.

THE NATURE OF THE WORK

Mechanical engineering is organized into three general areas: energy, manufacturing, and engineering design mechanics. Mechanical engineers are concerned with:

- The use of energy from natural sources and its economical conversion into other forms of useful energy
- The design and fabrication of machines to lighten the burden of human work
- Processing materials into products that are useful to people
- Creative planning, development, and operation of systems for using energy resources and machines
- The education and training of specialists, frequently called *technicians*, to deal with mechanical systems
- Acting as an interface between society and technology

The American Society of Mechanical Engineers has thirty-eight technical divisions, reflecting the diversity of disciplines, technologies, and industries. The areas covered include:

Advanced energy systems
Aerospace
Applied mechanics
Bioengineering
Computers and information in engineering
Design engineering
Dynamic systems and control
Electronic and photonic packaging
Environmental engineering
Fluids engineering
Fluid power systems and technology
Fuels and combustion technologies

Heat transfer
Information storage and processing systems
Internal combustion engine
International gas turbine institute
Management
Manufacturing engineering
Materials
Materials handling engineering
Microelectromechanical systems
Noise control and acoustics
Nondestructive evaluation engineering
Nuclear engineering
Ocean, offshore, and arctic engineering
Petroleum
Pipeline systems
Plant engineering and maintenance
Power
Pressure vessels and piping
Process industries
Rail transportation
Safety engineering and risk analysis
Solar energy
Solid waste processing
Technology and society
Textile engineering
Tribology

The Spectrum of Mechanical Engineering Functions

Figure 11.1 shows a listing of the major components of mechanical engineering activities. This broad spectrum includes most of the types of work engaged in by engineers after graduation. In actual life, the graduate may shift from one activity to another. For example, a graduate may start in the production area, then shift to the design area, later to testing, and then, in some cases, to technical sales. In small companies, one individual may handle several aspects of the business at the same time, as a designer, production supervisor, and testing engineer—all from the same desk.

Figure 11.1

Spectrum of activities engaged in by mechanical engineers

| Research | Development | Design | Testing | Manufacturing | Operation/Maintenance | Marketing/Sales | Administration |

As the spectrum implies, different talents and interests are required by different areas of the same company. For example, at the left end of the spectrum we find engineers who are science oriented, technically competent, and mathematically gifted. If those engineers consult or teach, they must also be able to deal with people and have skill in communicating ideas.

At the right-hand side of the spectrum, we find engineers who deal with materials, business matters, and people. Those involved as manufacturers' representatives or sales engineers or with legal aspects of engineering and business may not require the technical competence of a research engineer but should be knowledgeable about business, accounting, economics, and people.

In a spectrum of this sort, there is no higher or lower order. The left side is no more preferred than the right side.

Research

Research is the first step in solving a problem. The engineer will obtain data, devise new methods of calculation, and so acquire new knowledge.

Development

In development, the engineer takes the information and knowledge gained from the research and begins to expand it. At this stage, a simulation or experimental device might be produced and further extended into either a process or system that approximates a solution to the problem and fits the final need.

Design

In the design phase, the engineer actually conceptualizes the machine, the approach, or the system that will solve the problem. Careful documentation of all details is necessary to bring the solution from idea to reality. The solution is described quantitatively and put into equations or computer-aided design form.

Testing

To perform a test, the engineer will utilize either experimental devices or full-scale completed machines, system, or equipment. These devices will be operated to determine performance. At the same time, the mechanical engineer is checking to determine how much use or abuse the device can withstand, its relative strengths and weaknesses, and how to improve its performance. In essence, this phase of the mechanical engineer's work is to determine that whatever is being tested will perform as it is intended and can function in the environmental conditions that were anticipated in the design criteria.

Manufacturing

In the manufacturing stage the mechanical engineer must answer a series of questions. How is the product best manufactured? What is the most economical way of making it? What processes will be required? What are the skills and personnel needed to produce it? These questions are answered by a production engineer. The production engineer is the person who selects the equipment and machines and supervises arrangement and operation in detail. This engineer is also responsible for efficient, economical, and safe manufacturing.

Operation and Maintenance

Some equipment or systems require specialized knowledge and expertise above the level technicians usually have for operation and maintenance. These systems and equipment require the continual care only a mechanical engineer can provide. These duties might be mandated by law, as are the supervision and maintenance responsibilities for a nuclear or fossil fuel plant. Federal and state regulations require a mechanical engineer at such plants to perform certain specific tasks.

Marketing and Sales

When a firm offers a complex product or system, it can't rely only on a salesperson to present it to prospective clients. This is especially true in the case of systems and equipment that require formal technical backgrounds in order to understand and explain them. In this case, mechanical engineers would function as sales or marketing engineers, relying on their technical background and communications skills to demonstrate a product or a system to a customer. Often these engineers will work with the customer to modify the basic system or product design to meet the customer's specific requirement.

Administration

As in the other engineering disciplines, administration and management are logical stepping-stones for mechanical engineers. As engineers gain more experience and show an aptitude for supervising and coordinating activities and people, they gradually find themselves with more people to supervise and more responsibilities. At this point, the day-to-day technical aspects of the job are replaced with human problems. The engineer will be guiding, formulating policy, coordinating, and interacting with people more than machines.

The preceding descriptions are not intended to be complete, but rather to give a summary of the sorts of things mechanical engineers do.

Mechanical engineering demands an aptitude for and interest in the physical sciences and mathematics, and it requires the ability to apply these interests to benefit society and meet its needs.

THE SETTINGS IN WHICH MECHANICAL ENGINEERS WORK

There are over two hundred thousand mechanical engineers, and almost half of them are employed in the manufacturing sector. In fact, all large industries employ mechanical engineers. Traditional industries for mechanical engineers have included the automotive, industrial machinery, utilities, chemical, computer, manufacturing, mining, and petroleum industries. However, mechanical engineers are also employed in such industries as publishing and printing, oceanography, textiles, pharmaceuticals, apparel, soap and cosmetics, electronics, paper and wood products, and rubber and glass.

Some other areas of employment for mechanical engineers include materials, pollution control, electronic packaging, medicine, and aerospace. In addition, mechanical engineers do research and teach at colleges and universities. They also work at the federal, state, and local government levels and for consulting engineering firms. Some employers of mechanical engineers include:

Eaton Corporation
GE
Bechtel Corporation
Raytheon
Honeywell
Goodyear Tire and Rubber
General Motors
Ford Motor Company
Daimler Chrysler
Caterpillar
John Deere
Navistar International Corporation
NASA
U.S. Food and Drug Administration

EDUCATION AND OTHER QUALIFICATIONS

Mechanical engineers follow a very traditional engineering education process at the undergraduate level. Courses include the following.

- *Basic science.* Mathematics, physics, and life science provide a foundation for all engineering and technical courses.
- *Engineering sciences.* Engineering courses include solid mechanics, fluid mechanics, thermodynamics, heat transfer, finite element analysis, systems and controls, materials, electricity, and magnetism. In addition, some course work may be offered or required in the electrical and material engineering fields.
- *Design manufacturing.* An introduction to the process of joining ideas, imagination, and modeling to create components and systems.
- *Communications.* English, graphics, and computer languages.
- *Humanities.* Courses from one or more of the following: literature, sociology, history, psychology, economics, and philosophy. These courses are designed to round out engineers and better prepare

them for their role in society through knowledge and
understanding of their culture, themselves, and one another.

OUTLOOK FOR THE FUTURE

According to the U.S. Bureau of Labor Statistics, the demand for improved
machinery, machine tools, and complex manufacturing processes is creating a growing demand for mechanical engineers. In addition, new technologies in microelectromechancial systems, computer technology, and
bioengineering are creating opportunities for mechanical engineers.

Other opportunities are expected to be in the engineering services area
(engineering consulting firms) as manufacturing companies contract out
design, development, and testing work to solve engineering problems. This
area is expected to grow more rapidly through 2010. In addition, as the
workforce ages and engineers retire, more opportunities for mechanical
engineers will be created.

EARNINGS

Mechanical engineers had a median annual salary of $58,710 in 2000,
according to the U.S. Bureau of Labor Statistics. The lowest 10 percent of
mechanical engineers earned less than $38,770, and the highest 10 percent
earned more than $88,610.

For those graduating from college in 2001, the National Association of
Colleges and Employers reported that mechanical engineering bachelor's-
degree candidates received starting offers averaging $48,426 a year, that
master's-degree candidates received offers averaging $55,994, and Ph.D.
candidates received offers averaging $72,096.

ADDITIONAL SOURCES OF INFORMATION

Air Conditioning and Refrigeration Institute (ARI)
4301 North Fairfax Drive, Suite 425
Arlington, VA 22203
ari.org

American Boiler Manufacturers Association (ABMA)
950 North Glebe Road, Suite 160
Arlington, VA 22203
abma.com

American Consulting Engineers Council (ACEC)
1015 Fifteenth Street NW, Suite 802
Washington, DC 20005
acec.org

American Design Drafting Association (ADDA)
P.O. Box 799
Rockville, MD 20848-0799
adda.org

American Nuclear Society (ANS)
555 North Kensington Avenue
LaGrange Park, IL 60526
ans.org

American Society of Body Engineers (ASBE)
2122 Fifteen Mile Road, Suite F
Sterling Heights, MI 48310
asbe.com

American Society for Nondestructive Testing (ASNT)
1711 Arlingate Lane
P.O. Box 28518
Columbus, OH 43228-0518
asnt.org

American Society of Heating, Refrigerating and Air-Conditioning
    Engineers (ASHRAE)
1791 Tullie Circle NE
Atlanta, GA 30329
ashrae.org

American Society of Mechanical Engineers (ASME)
Three Park Avenue
New York, NY 10016
asme.org

Mechanical Contractors Association of America, Inc.
1385 Picard Drive
Rockville, MD 20850
mcaa.org

Robotic Industries Association (RIA)
900 Victors Way
P.O. Box 3724
Ann Arbor, MI 48106
robotics.org

Sheet Metal and Air Conditioning Contractors National Association
   (SMACNA)
4201 Lafayette Center Drive
Chantilly, VA 20151-1209
smacna.org

Society for the Advancement of Material and Process Engineering
   (SAMPE)
1161 Parkview Drive
Covina, CA 91724-3748
et.byu.edu/org/sampe

Society of Automotive Engineers, Inc. (SAE)
400 Commonwealth Drive
Warrendale, PA 15096-0001
sae.org

Society of Manufacturing Engineers (SME)
One SME Drive
P.O. Box 930
Dearborn, MI 48121-0930
sme.org

C H A P T E R

AEROSPACE ENGINEERING*

Aerospace engineering, like the entire field of aerospace, has grown far beyond its original concerns with aeronautics and space. Aerospace professionals confront many challenges and even address problems closer to earth in the areas of mass transportation, environmental pollution, and medical science. That is why it is possible to prepare for a career in aerospace engineering either by pursuing a degree in mechanical, electrical, chemical, or materials science engineering or by pursuing aerospace engineering as a college major in its own right. Whichever educational path is chosen, aerospace engineers find themselves on the leading edge of technology, and their solutions to problems encountered in exploring space also provide solutions to problems closer to home.

THE NATURE OF THE WORK

By definition, the aerospace engineer is involved in all phases of research and development in aeronautics and astronautics. An aeronautical engineer works specifically with aircraft or aeronautics. An astronautical engineer works specifically with spacecraft or astronautics.

---

*Content contributed by the American Institute of Aeronautics and Astronautics, Inc.

As technology races forward, the industry that once built aircraft and then spacecraft is now building aerospace craft, such as the Space Shuttle or X-33. Thus, two interrelated industries are merging into one mature "aerospace" industry.

Aerospace engineering involves about seven major divisions—each with its supporting technology—which often cross the lines of other engineering fields. These major divisions include propulsion, fluid mechanics, thermodynamics, structures, celestial mechanics, acoustics, and guidance and control.

Propulsion

The study of propulsion involves the analysis of matter as it flows through various devices such as combustion chambers, diffusers, nozzles, and turbochargers. A vehicle's propulsion system is the primary force responsible for performance.

Fluid Mechanics

Fluid mechanics deals with the motion of gases and liquids as well as with the effects of the motion on bodies in the medium. Engineers working in the division of fluid dynamics called aerodynamics are concerned with the determination of a vehicle's shape and configuration.

Thermodynamics

The science of thermodynamics is concerned with the relationship between heat and work. The principles of thermodynamics interest aerospace engineers studying thermal balance within vehicles, thermal effects produced by high-speed reentry into the atmosphere, and environmental control systems.

Structures

The science of structures develops advanced techniques in the areas of structural analysis, dynamic loads, aeroelasticity, and design criteria. The engineer in this field must answer two questions about any framework: (1)

Is it strong enough to withstand the loads applied to it? and (2) Is it stiff enough to avoid excessive deformation and deflections?

Celestial Mechanics

The science of celestial mechanics is concerned with the motion of particles in space. These particles can represent rockets, planets, missiles, or spacecraft. When engineers prepare a space mission, a major concern is determining the paths of the rockets and planets. Their calculations, facilitated by banks of computer devices, take into consideration the propulsion systems, optimum programs for fuel or propellant utilization, optimal trajectories, transfer orbits, and the potential effects of thrust misalignment.

Acoustics

Acoustics deals with the production and behavior of sound. Some of the problems aerospace engineers address include internal noise generated from stators, rotors, fans, and combustion chambers. They also study sonic booms and their effects on the urban and rural environment.

Guidance and Control

Guidance and control systems automate the control, maneuverability, and path systems of a space vehicle in order to fulfill its mission objectives. Examples of systems on a more conventional level include the ILS (instrument landing system), which permits aircraft to land day or night in all kinds of weather. Similar systems also provide guidance and control for submarines.

THE SETTINGS IN WHICH AEROSPACE ENGINEERS WORK

The settings in which aerospace engineers work can vary widely. The environment could be an office, a laboratory, an airfield, or even outer space, depending on the career goals and interests of an individual.

Aerospace engineers who do cost analysis, preliminary design, or pure research would most likely work in an office or library. However, if an aerospace engineer were doing flight-testing, actual design, or field service, you would probably find him or her in a laboratory or out "in the field." If an engineer were doing work on or for satellites, space shuttles, or the International Space Station, then space could very well be his or her work atmosphere from time to time.

Many aerospace engineers are employed in the aerospace industries, including companies such as:

BAE Systems
The Boeing Company
Bombardier Inc.
Eaton Corporation
General Dynamics Corporation
Goodrich Corporation
Honeywell International Inc.
ITT Industries, Inc.
Lockheed Martin Corporation
Northrop Grumman Corporation
Raytheon Company
Teledyne Technologies
United Technologies Corporation

Many of these companies receive major contracts from the U.S. Department of Defense and commercial airline companies. Other aerospace engineers are employed in government agencies, particularly in the U.S. Department of Defense and the National Aeronautics and Space Administration (NASA).

EDUCATION AND OTHER QUALIFICATIONS

Experts agree that junior high school is the best time to begin planning for a career in aerospace engineering. Most colleges and universities offering programs in aerospace engineering expect the students they admit to have taken the following courses in high school:

- English (Foreign students may be allowed to take an English class while attending school, but will most likely be expected to take the TOEFL exam.)
- Math (algebra, geometry, trigonometry). Most universities will start with a calculus class freshman year—if your high school offers calculus, take it.
- Science (biology, chemistry, and physics)
- History (three years including social studies)

Many high schools will offer advanced placement (AP) classes. Anyone intending to attend a university at all should attempt to take any AP classes available.

Many colleges vary in their curricula, but most will expect an aeronautics/astronautics (aero/astro) student to take the following (some schools do not offer an aero/astro degree, but have tracks within the mechanical engineering department to prepare students to enter the aero/astro field):

- English (English is the official language of scientists. Almost every technical or science conference will have the presentations given in English.)
- Technical writing
- Math (analytical geometry, calculus [two years], matrices and nonlinear algebra, linear and nonlinear differential equations)
- Basic sciences (physics and laboratory [two years], chemistry and laboratory)
- Statics and dynamics (study of any and all forces on systems or objects that are stationary [statics] or moving [dynamics])
- Electronics (introduction)
- Structural analysis
- Aerodynamics/fluid flow
- Heat transfer
- Material sciences

In addition to these basics, students are expected to take several technical electives. Some of these can be on any technical topic, but three to four technical electives will be aero/astro specific.

Some of these technical electives are:

- Orbital mechanics
- Electromagnetic fields
- Flight vehicle design
- Spacecraft design
- Vehicle stability and control
- Space structures
- Flight mechanics
- Trajectory dynamics
- Telecommunications
- Propulsion
- Gas dynamics

Special Programs to Explore Aerospace Engineering Careers While in School

There are many opportunities for students to enhance their education with other activities. One of these ways is by taking part in cooperative engineering education (co-op). Many colleges and universities offer co-ops. The university often has an office dedicated to this. In fact, many schools are beginning to require students to do co-ops. The American Institute of Aeronautics and Astronautics (AIAA) website (aiaa.org) links to other websites that offer co-ops and internships.

NASA also offers several programs to help students, including co-ops as well as a variety of competitions. Some of the NASA competitions allow students the opportunity to fly on the KC-135A, also known as the Vomit Comet. The KC-135A flies a series of parabolic patterns that allow the students to perform experiments in zero or microgravity.

The American Institute of Aeronautics and Astronautics has student branches at over 150 universities throughout the world. The student branches often have many local activities to help enhance aerospace education. These activities include local speakers from AIAA professional sections, mentoring with local high schools and elementary schools, trips to and tours of aerospace industries, and a variety of others. The student branches also take part in a regional student conference.

Regional student conferences are organized by a host branch, with help from a faculty advisor and AIAA headquarters. The students prepare a paper on a subject of their choosing and submit it. The host school supplies a panel of aeronautical and astronautical professionals to judge the papers on their technical content. A panel of judges is also supplied to hear the papers at a presentation.

This allows the students to get a real feel of presenting to their peers. Although not everyone in the aerospace industry presents papers at conferences, almost all go to conferences. The student conferences allow the students to become comfortable in a conference atmosphere. Also, many professional aerospace people and AIAA members attend these conferences, so the students are able to start networking before they ever get out of college.

The winners of the regional conferences are supported to the AIAA Foundation National Student Conference held in conjunction with the AIAA annual Aerospace Sciences Meeting.

If writing a paper isn't what the student would like to do to enhance his or her education, the AIAA Foundation also sponsors design competitions. These competitions allow students to design an actual product and get used to reading requests for proposals (RFPs) and preparing a proposal in response. The AIAA Foundation offers several different topics for students to choose from. There are team graduate, team undergraduate, and individual competitions. These competitions not only allow the students to understand and do actual design, but they have monetary value as well. First place receives $2,500, and a representative of the team is appointed to a technical conference to present the team's work. Second place receives $1,500, and third receives $1,000.

For those students that like a little more hands-on type of work, the AIAA Foundation also sponsors a design/build/fly competition. In this competition, students design a radio-controlled airplane to perform a specific function. The function could be to carry tennis balls in a certain pattern, to fly a particular pattern with as many softballs or as much weight as possible, etc. The students write a short report discussing the design process that they went through to determine how and with what they would build their plane. Then, after they have built it, they bring their plane to a central location (either Patuxent River, Maryland, or Wichita, Kansas) and fly against other teams in a "flyoff." The total score for each team is a combination of the report, the design, and the flyoff.

This event is very popular among the AIAA student membership. There are usually over twenty-five teams that participate. Teams from outside the United States compete as well. Turkey and Italy often send teams to participate in the competition. Many people come just to watch the competition. It isn't unheard of to have 250 spectators at the three-day event.

OUTLOOK FOR THE FUTURE

Aerospace engineering is significantly impacted by government policies in the area of defense and space programs. While there is always a need for aerospace engineers, the availability of federal funding for research and development and production varies greatly. Therefore, the aerospace industry has a cyclical atmosphere, as many disciplines do.

As a result of the terrorist attacks on September 11, 2001, the aeronautical and astronautical community will be making significant changes to current vehicles and technologies as well as developing new ones. This means opportunities in the industry. Therefore, the outlook for opportunities in aerospace and aeronautical engineering are good.

EARNINGS

Today, aerospace engineering graduates can expect starting salary offers between $33,000 and $48,000. Using standard increases and promotion figures, this means that aerospace engineers who have kept current with technologies in the field may be looking at an income of $105,000 to $145,000 annually in the later stages of their career.

In 2000, the U.S. Bureau of Labor Statistics published the median annual earnings in the employment sectors that hired the largest numbers of aerospace engineers in 2000. They were:

Federal government $74,170
Search and navigation equipment $71,020
Aircraft and parts $68,230
Guided missiles, space vehicles, and parts $65,830

In 2001, the National Association of Colleges and Employers reported that bachelor's-degree candidates in aerospace engineering received starting offers averaging $46,918 a year, master's-degree candidates received starting offers averaging $59,955, and Ph.D. candidates received starting offers averaging $64,167.

The Department of Labor offers salary information at the following websites: bls.gov/oes/2000/oes172011.htm and bls.gov/bls/blswage.htm.

ADDITIONAL SOURCES OF INFORMATION

American Institute of Aeronautics and Astronautics, Inc. (AIAA)
1801 Alexander Bell Drive, Suite 500
Reston, VA 20191
aiaa.org

Aerospace Industries Association
1250 Eye Street NW, Suite 1200
Washington, DC 20005-3924
aia-aerospace.org

American Astronomical Society
2000 Florida Avenue NW, Suite 400
Washington, DC 20009-1231
aas.org

International Astronautical Federation
3/5 rue Mario Nikis
75015 Paris, France
iafastro.com

International Council of Aeronautical Sciences
66, route de Verneuil
BP 3002
France
icas.org

Canadian Aeronautics and Space Institute
1685, chemin Russell Road, Unité 1R
Ottawa, ON K1G 0N1
Canada
casi.ca

NASA
nasa.gov

NASA's educational outreach is a good source of information. The NASA Why? Files (http://whyfiles.larc.nasa.gov/treehouse.html) is a website dedicated to students interested in aerospace.

Currently AIAA has an educational partnership with NASA, and manages and organizes NASA's space station utilization conferences.

AIAA also has a contract with the Federal Aviation Administration (FAA) as a result of the September 11, 2001, attack. The FAA received thousands and thousands of E-mails, letters, and faxes about how to improve security. AIAA is working with the FAA to sort through and organize all of these ideas.

AIAA has a booklet called *Careers Within Your Lifetime.* This booklet is aimed at eighth graders. It allows students to find out what they can do as an aerospace engineer and how to plan for it. It gives a general idea of what classes students need to take in high school and college to receive a degree in aerospace engineering.

C H A P T E R

13

AGRICULTURAL ENGINEERING

Agricultural engineering is a discipline that probably has the closest relationship to the environment of almost any engineering discipline. To ensure tomorrow's food production, agricultural engineers work to protect today's environment. Therefore, agricultural engineering can either be pursued as a major in its own right, at universities that offer degrees in agricultural engineering, or as a specialty in such majors as civil engineering, chemical engineering, bioengineering, or mechanical or electrical engineering.

Agricultural productivity is a key measure of an agricultural engineer's performance. As agricultural engineers develop new tools, it becomes increasingly easier and more practical to produce, process, and distribute food and fibers.

The work of agricultural engineers is increasingly important, as the food industry contributes $400 billion to the gross national product (GNP) of the United States and employs approximately twenty-five thousand engineers. Likewise, the construction industry uses more tonnage of wood, a biological material with unique properties, than all metals combined. In addition, over two hundred industrial products, not including pharmaceuticals, are produced with cell cultures that come from plants, animals, and microorganisms.

THE NATURE OF THE WORK

Agricultural engineers utilize scientific and engineering principles to design processes, systems, and equipment to manage the resources that provide us with food, fiber, and timber. These skills are applied across the vast food-production chain, from the preservation of food products to the protection of natural resources. These resources include soil, water, air, energy, and engineering materials.

Some agricultural engineers apply biotechnology, computer science, and knowledge-based programs to control equipment used in the production of food. For example, computerized systems such as the Global Positioning Systems (GPS) and the Geographic Information Systems (GIS) accurately guide the application of seeds, fertilizers, water, and chemicals by farm equipment that has onboard computers, laser sensing, and robotics. Other engineers work with environmental concerns such as air and water quality and soil erosion and loss. Still others develop renewable energy from sources that augment and conserve fossil fuels.

Today agricultural engineering can be considered in four major categories: bioprocess engineering, land and water resources engineering, bioenvironmental engineering, and off-road equipment engineering.

Bioprocess Engineering

Bioprocess engineering designs, develops, and manufactures value-added products through further processing of agricultural materials. Engineers work with the production of food, feed, pharmaceuticals, nutraceuticals, fuels, lubricants, polymers, and chemicals. They use biological, thermal, chemical, and mechanical processing to develop new products and to design processing systems. Those systems include, but are not limited to, process control development, bioreactor design, scale-up of processes, upstream and downstream processing, and organic waste utilization. Some of the specializations of bioprocess engineering are food process engineering, primary processing, bioprocessing, bioremediation, and timber engineering.

Food Process Engineering

Engineers in this area design the processes used to manufacture food products to ensure that our food is safe and of the highest quality.

Primary Processing

Engineers specializing in primary processing make use of knowledge of how biological materials are changed by natural enzymes and surface microorganisms so that raw materials can be harvested from land and water and stored to later become foodstocks for a wide range of processing activities.

Bioprocessing

In bioprocessing the engineer designs products, and then separates and purifies them through processes and control systems that implement cell-culture manufacturing, such as fermentation, which uses enzymes to accomplish various goals.

Bioremediation

In bioremediation the engineer designs and implements procedures that use carefully selected organisms (or genetically manipulated organisms) to break down toxic materials in order to restore the productivity of land and water.

Timber Engineering

Engineers in this area develop engineered wood products such as trusses, laminated beams, and wall panels.

Land and Water Resources Engineering

The purpose of land and water resources engineering is to manage production of biological materials while protecting the environment. Engineers who work in this area protect and preserve the environment through conservation of natural resources and pollution control. They apply biological, ecological, and engineering principles to develop production systems that conserve natural resources and minimize pollution through erosion control, ground- and surface water quality management, storm water management, land development, and organic waste management. Some of the specializations of land and water resources engineering are erosion control, site development planning, water quality, waste management, bioenvironmental engineering, and off-road equipment engineering.

Erosion Control

Engineers in this area design terraces, meadow strips, and drainage systems to maintain productivity of agricultural land and water quality because runoff from agricultural land can erode topsoil and fill streams with sediment.

Site Development Planning

In this specialty, engineers recommend and/or implement needed controls for storm water runoff or to improve water quality in order to positively impact surrounding biological systems for agricultural production.

Water Quality

Engineers concerned with water quality analyze and design mechanisms by which water flow interacts with soil microorganisms and plants.

Waste Management

Engineers in this area devise methods to return waste from animal production facilities and water treatment plants to the land in a sustainable manner, improve the ability of crops to use nutrients, and avoid contamination of surface and groundwater.

Bioenvironmental Engineering

In bioenvironmental engineering, the engineer is concerned with design and development of building layout, structural analysis, indoor air quality and ventilation, plumbing and electrical systems, foundations of structures, the treatment and handling of waste products, and animal and plant responses to the environment.

Off-Road Equipment Engineering

Engineers in off-road equipment engineering take part in the design, development, and manufacture of machines, engines, and machine components and are concerned with machine element analysis and guidance and control of machines that move, till, or otherwise interact with soils.

The University of Illinois Department of Agricultural Engineering identifies at least nineteen different job functions performed by agricultural engineers. They are:

1. Buildings and building products
2. Machinery and machine components
3. Fluid power
4. Off-road machines
5. Combustion engines
6. Energy utilization
7. Electrical power distribution
8. Controls
9. Alternate energy systems
10. Natural resources
11. Water quality and supply
12. Waste handling and treatment
13. Land and water management
14. Electronics, instrumentation, and controls
15. Biosensors
16. Machine vision
17. Food and biological products
18. Shipping and storage
19. Food processing and handling

THE SETTINGS IN WHICH AGRICULTURAL ENGINEERS WORK

Agricultural engineers are employed in many settings. Some of the settings include engineering and environmental consulting firms, where they validate processes used in food and drug industries, prepare land use plans and environmental impact assessments, or build agricultural waste handling facilities and equipment.

Opportunities for agricultural engineers also exist in government agencies at local, state, and federal levels. Some examples at the state and federal levels are the Department of Conservation and Recreation, the Environmental Protection Agency, the Natural Resources Conservation

Services, the Department of Agriculture, the Army Corps of Engineers, the Food and Drug Administration, and the Geological Survey.

For those in the bioprocessing area of agricultural engineering, opportunities exist in the food, pharmaceutical, and biotech industries and with numerous other companies that manufacture bio-based industrial products. Some employers in this area include:

A. O. Smith Corp.
Andrews Environmental Engineering, Inc.
Archer Daniels Midland (ADM)
Cargill
Case Corp.
Caterpillar Tractor, Inc.
Daimler Chrysler Corp.
Cummings Engine Co., Inc.
Deere and Co.
Del Monte Foods, Inc.
Dole Foods, Inc.
FMC Corp.
Ford Motor Co.
General Mills, Inc.
General Motors Corp.
Kraft General Foods
Morton Buildings, Inc.
Quaker Oats Co. (recently merged with Pepsico)
The Pillsbury Company
Trane Corp.
U.S. Armed Forces
U.S. Bureau of Reclamation

EDUCATION AND OTHER QUALIFICATIONS

Agricultural engineering degree programs are now offered under names other than agricultural engineering. Some are called biological systems engineering, bioresource engineering, bioenvironmental engineering, forest engineering, or food process engineering.

Nonetheless, preparation for studying any of the programs related to agricultural engineering begins in junior high school. At this level, it is important to take the appropriate math and science courses that prepare someone for three years of high school science, including chemistry and physics, and four years of high school mathematics, including trigonometry and calculus.

While the course work required for a bachelor's degree in agricultural engineering varies slightly from school to school, most programs include course work in mechanization, soil and water resource management, food process engineering, industrial microbiology, or pest management. In addition, most agricultural engineers take courses in computer science and engineering design. These courses prepare them for the senior capstone course where students design, build, and test new agricultural processes, products, or systems.

Students interested in the medical or veterinary fields can usually follow the general agricultural engineering curriculum and select additional biology and chemistry courses as electives to prepare for medical or veterinary school. Agricultural engineering careers in business, industry, and government require a minimum of a bachelor's degree in an engineering field related to agricultural engineering. Positions in teaching or research require additional college education at the master's and Ph.D. level. Regardless of the work setting, agricultural engineers need to continually update their knowledge and skills through continuing education courses and/or advanced degrees in order to remain current in the field.

The American Society of Agricultural Engineering's website (asae.org) provides a complete list of colleges and universities offering programs related to agricultural engineering.

Special Programs to Explore Agricultural Engineering

The American Society of Agricultural Engineering (ASAE) sponsors two student design competitions. They are the National Student Design Competition and the Environmental Design Student Competition. The goal of both competitions is to be educational and fun for students interested in pursuing careers in agricultural engineering.

In the ASAE National Student Design Competition, teams of students design a one-quarter-scale multistage tractor, which is used to pull a progressive sled. In this competition, each entry is judged for its written design report, team presentation, individual design, and performance in competition.

Another ASAE competition is the Environmental Design Student Competition. Every year, teams of students are given a different problem to solve. An example of the type of problem that students are asked to address in this competition is the "Optimized Bench-Scale Treatment Plant for Sugary Waste." In this design competition, students were told that a confectionery plant was projected to produce a certain level of liquid wastewater and that the municipal wastewater treatment authority could not accept the entire load. The plant owners were asked to install technology that would reduce the load by at least 60 percent. Student teams each produced a system design for the installation of the new technology and the construction phases of the project. The winning design had to show excellence in full-scale design and an understanding of real-world issues, including sensitivity to economic, ethical, safety, and regulatory issues.

OUTLOOK FOR THE FUTURE

ASAE states that there is a solid future for agricultural engineers. The society reports that there is a steady job market, competitive salaries, and interesting work that benefits society in this field. In addition, according to the U.S. Bureau of Labor Statistics, the employment of agricultural engineers is expected to increase through 2010. In large part, increases in opportunities will be due to the retirement of a growing number of agricultural engineers. It will also be due to increased demand for more efficiently produced agricultural products and the conservation of resources.

EARNINGS

The National Association of Colleges and Employers' 2001 salary survey reported that the average agricultural engineering bachelor's-degree candidate received starting salary offers averaging $46,065 a year, and the average master's-degree candidate received starting salary offers averaging $49,808.

In 2000, the U.S. Bureau of Labor Statistics reported that the median annual earnings of agricultural engineers were $55,850, with the lowest 10 percent earning less than $33,660 and the highest 10 percent earning more than $91,600.

ADDITIONAL SOURCE OF INFORMATION

American Society of Agricultural Engineers (ASAE)
2950 Niles Road
St. Joseph, MI 49085-9659
asae.org

C H A P T E R

AUTOMOTIVE ENGINEERING

Automotive engineering involves the design, development, testing, and manufacture of vehicles and their components. It is a field wide open to the inquisitive engineer who wishes to be involved in a broad variety of disciplines and their applications. Automotive engineering is one of those disciplines that can either be pursued as a specialty area within mechanical, electrical, industrial, chemical, or materials science engineering or it can be pursued at a college or university that offers automotive engineering as a major in its own right.

THE NATURE OF THE WORK

Jobs in the field of automotive engineering include the application of mechanical engineering, chemical engineering, electrical engineering, materials engineering, aerospace engineering, computer engineering, and civil engineering. Additionally, automotive engineering makes use of virtually every other field of pure or applied science and technology.

Automotive engineers not only design, develop, test, and manufacture passenger cars and trucks, they are also involved with such things as emissions safety, fuels and lubricants, construction and industrial machinery, electrical equipment, electronic systems, engine, body chassis, hydraulics, materials, occupant restraint, human factors, tires, wheels, transmissions, suspensions, and aerodynamics.

Automotive engineers work to improve vehicle efficiency, performance, reliability, and safety. Their responsibilities can include:

- Analysis of vehicle structures, using finite element analysis methods
- Precision mechanical designs, using two-dimensional layout and detail drawings and computer-aided design software, such as AutoCad or ProEngineering
- Failure analysis
- Testing of vehicle and engine electrical/electronic systems
- Development of new or modified component designs
- Creating prototype design drawings (including three-dimensional and wireframe drawings) using CATIA software

THE SETTINGS IN WHICH AUTOMOTIVE ENGINEERS WORK

Automotive engineers are employed in the automobile manufacturing industry at companies such as Ford Motor Company, General Motors, and Daimler Chrysler. However, many more automotive engineers are employed in automotive support services such as the electronic components industry, the tire industry, the fabricated plastics and metals industries, and the transportation industry.

EDUCATION AND OTHER QUALIFICATIONS

Like all other areas of engineering, automotive engineers should begin preparation as early as junior high school by taking as much math and science as possible. Although no four-year, accredited colleges or universities award degrees in automotive engineering, many of the traditional areas of engineering (mechanical engineering, chemical engineering, electrical engineering, materials engineering, aerospace engineering) provide related course offerings. Colleges and universities involved in automotive engineering will usually have active student chapters of the Society of Automotive Engineers (SAE).

There are more than 380 SAE chapters at universities worldwide. Over fifteen thousand student members participate in engineering projects, attend free section meetings, and benefit from free technical papers and publications. Many students build vehicles to compete in some of SAE's annual collegiate design competitions.

Special Programs for Automotive Engineering Students

The Society of Automotive Engineers offers competitions that challenge students' knowledge, creativity, and imagination. These competitions are Mini Baja, Aero Design, Formula SAE, Supermileage, Walking Machine Challenge, and Clean Snowmobile Challenge.

1. SAE's Mini Baja competition consists of three regional competitions where teams of engineering students design and build off-road vehicles that will survive the severe punishment of rough terrain and water.

2. SAE's Aero Design competition provides an opportunity for teams of engineering students to conceive, design, fabricate, and test a radio-controlled aircraft that can take off and land while carrying the maximum cargo.

3. Formula SAE competition provides an opportunity for teams of engineering students to design, fabricate, and compete with small formula-style race cars. The vehicles are judged in three different categories: static inspection and engineering design, solo performance trails, and high-performance track endurance.

4. Supermileage competition provides an opportunity for engineering students to design and build a one-person, fuel-efficient vehicle based on a small four-cycle engine. All vehicles are powered by a two-horsepower Briggs & Stratton engine in order to create a challenging engineering design test.

5. Walking Machine Challenge provides teams of engineering students an opportunity to gain design experience while building a machine with independent legs that walks, climbs, and maneuvers around objects.

6. Clean Snowmobile Challenge provides teams of engineering students an opportunity to redesign a snowmobile to improve its emissions and noise while maintaining its performance

characteristics. Entries are judged on emissions, noise, fuel economy/range, acceleration, power, and design.

OUTLOOK FOR THE FUTURE

The employment outlook for automotive engineers is somewhat uncertain. On the one hand, the influx of imported automobiles has made the U.S. marketplace soft. On the other hand, a revitalization and reindustrialization of the U.S. auto industry could result in more opportunities and challenges for today's automotive engineers as U.S. auto manufacturers seek to reestablish their dominance in the field.

EARNINGS

Because automotive engineers have degrees in traditional engineering disciplines, the reader should consult the specific chapters on the individual engineering fields about the starting earnings and median salaries in each area.

ADDITIONAL SOURCES OF INFORMATION

American Society of Body Engineers (ASBE)
2122 Fifteen Mile Road, Suite F
Sterling Heights, MI 48310
asbe.com

Society of Automotive Engineers, Inc. (SAE)
400 Commonwealth Drive
Warrendale, PA 15096-0001
sae.org

CHAPTER 15

BIOMEDICAL ENGINEERING

Biomedical engineers apply their knowledge of engineering and human anatomy to the discovery and maintenance of systems and equipment used to assist medical and other health-care professionals. Some of the many contributions of biomedical engineers include the development of:

- Miniature devices to deliver medications or inhibit growth of life-threatening cells at precise, targeted locations in order to promote healing or inhibit disease formation and progression
- Artificial biomaterials to replace bones, cartilages, ligaments, tendons, and spinal discs
- Automated monitors used by doctors to monitor surgical and intensive care patients and to monitor the unborn fetus in pregnant women, and by astronauts in space and deep-sea divers to monitor bodily functions under unusual circumstances
- Artificial hearts and heart valves, joint replacements, hearing aids, cardiac pacemakers, artificial kidneys, blood oxygenators, synthetic blood vessels, and prosthetic devices such as artificial arms and legs
- Advanced therapeutic and surgical devices such as laser systems for eye surgery and automated delivery of insulin
- Customized software to control medical instruments and to conduct data acquisition and analysis

• Medical imaging systems (MRIs and ultrasound), which are noninvasive diagnostic procedures, making them less painful for patients

Biomedical engineering is an engineering field that can either be pursued as a specialty within an engineering discipline such as electrical, mechanical, computer, chemical, or materials science engineering or it can be pursued as a major in its own right at those institutions that offer a specific preparation in bioengineering or biomedical engineering.

THE NATURE OF THE WORK

Biomedical engineers use their knowledge of science and engineering to analyze and solve problems in biology and medicine. Their work provides continued advancement of the health-care system through the design and improvement of instruments, devices, and software. It is a field of continual change and rapid advancement of technology.

Like other engineers, biomedical engineers work in teams. However, their teams tend to be made up of other health-care professionals including physicians, nurses, therapists, and technicians. According to the Whitaker Foundation, a funding organization for biomedical engineering research and education, some of the well-established specialty areas within the field of biomedical engineering are:

Bioinstrumentation
Biomaterials
Biomechanics
Cellular, tissue, and genetic engineering
Clinical engineering
Medical imaging
Orthopedic bioengineering
Rehabilitation engineering
Systems physiology

Biomedical engineers usually function as part of a medical team and are often the only professional engineer on the team. In many cases biomedical engineers provide the technical interface between the manufacturer and the user of medical equipment. Therefore, their interdisciplinary background and their engineering expertise is relied upon heavily. Biomedical engineers assess requirements and then research, design, and fabricate electronic instruments, software applications, or mechanical devices to meet specific requirements. The role of the biomedical engineer is one of the most exciting and rewarding of engineering opportunities.

Bioinstrumentation Engineers

Bioinstrumentation engineers develop devices used in diagnosis and treatment of disease. Computers are essential to bioinstrumentation, ranging from microprocessors in instruments performing small tasks to microcomputers that process large amounts of information in medical imaging.

Biomaterials Engineers

Biomaterials engineers research, identify, and develop properties and behavior of living tissue and artificial materials used in implant materials to assure that the materials are nontoxic, noncarcinogenic, chemically inert, stable, and mechanically strong enough for a lifetime of use. Certain metal alloys, ceramics, polymers, and composites have been used as implantable materials, and new materials will be developed in the future.

Biomechanics Engineers

Biomechanics engineers apply classical mechanics (statics, dynamics, fluids, solids, thermodynamics, and continuum mechanics) to the study of motion, material deformation, and flow of fluids within the body.

Cellular, Tissue, and Genetics Engineers

Cellular, tissue, and genetics engineers work at the microscopic level. They use their knowledge of anatomy, biochemistry, and mechanics of cellular and subcellular structures to understand disease and to intervene at specific sites.

Clinical Engineers

Clinical engineers purchase advanced medical instruments for hospital settings and work with physicians to adapt the instruments to meet the specific needs of physicians and the hospital. They also develop and maintain computer databases of medical instrumentation and equipment records.

Medical Imaging Engineers

Medical imaging engineers use knowledge of physical phenomena such as sound, radiation, and magnetism to design and develop equipment that generates images to be used for diagnostic purposes.

Orthopedic Bioengineers

Orthopedic bioengineers apply engineering and computational mechanics to understanding the function of bones, joints, and muscles, and for the design of artificial joint replacements.

Rehabilitation Engineers

Rehabilitation engineers are involved in the design and development of prosthetics and other assistive devices that enhance sitting and positioning, mobility, and communication.

Systems Physiology Engineers

Systems physiology engineers use strategies, techniques, and tools to understand the function of living organisms ranging from bacteria to humans. Computer modeling is used in the analysis of experimental data and in formulating mathematical descriptions of physiological events.

THE SETTINGS IN WHICH BIOMEDICAL ENGINEERS WORK

According to the Whitaker Foundation, "Biomedical engineers are employed in universities, in industry, in hospitals, in research facilities of educational and medical institutions, in teaching, and in government regulatory

Figure 15.1

Engineering Career Areas in Biomedical and Bioengineering

Discovery Research	Feasibility Research	Preclinical Trials	Clinical Trials	Premarket Approval	Large-Scale Manufacturing	Marketing	Technical Sales	Distribution

agencies." In 2000, the U.S. Bureau of Labor Statistics counted about seven thousand biomedical engineering positions, with one-third of those being in the manufacturing industry, primarily medical instrumentation and supplies. The roles the biomedical engineers play in industry can range from feasibility research to distribution. Figure 15.1 shows the range of industry opportunities for biomedical engineers.

In addition to the large proportion of biomedical engineers who go on to pursue medical degrees, a significant number of biomedical engineers are employed in hospitals. Not all biomedical engineers find themselves in clinical situations. For every engineer working in a hospital, there are probably five engaged in industry. These are the engineers who design and investigate new techniques and technology, taking a problem and turning it into an opportunity and then a solution.

These engineers can also be found in an academic or pure research setting, taking their in-depth knowledge of electronics and combining it with medicine to provide the means for even greater enrichment of human life.

EDUCATION AND OTHER QUALIFICATIONS

The recommended high school preparation for majoring in biomedical engineering is the same as that for any other engineering discipline, except that life science courses should also be included. Advanced placement (AP) courses in these areas would be strongly suggested.

At the college level, there are basically two types of biomedical curricula. The first leads to a bachelor's degree in biomedical engineering. The second leads to a bachelor's degree in a traditional engineering field, such as mechanical, electrical, or chemical engineering, where the student elects to take courses in a biomedical option. These courses supplement the regular engineering curriculum. Biomedical engineers are educated not only in the traditional engineering areas, but also in the biological disciplines of anatomy, biophysics, pharmacology, physiology, neurophysiology, and organic and biological chemistry. A list of academic programs in biomedical engineering is available from the Whitaker Foundation's website at whitaker.org/glance/programs.html. In addition, the "Biomedical Engineering Academic Program Annual Report" is available from BMEnet at http://bme.www.ecn.purdue.edu/bme/academic/grand.html.

Because industrial need for biomedical engineers is typically concentrated at the graduate level, a large percentage of biomedical engineers continue their studies beyond the undergraduate level. A high percentage of undergraduates go on to graduate or professional school immediately after graduation. In fact, the proportion of students enrolling in medical school is generally higher than the proportion entering industry or graduate programs in biomedical engineering.

OUTLOOK FOR THE FUTURE

The number of biomedical engineering jobs is expected to increase by over 31 percent through 2010. This increase is double the rate of all other jobs combined, according to the U.S. Department of Labor. The Whitaker Foundation's funding of more collegiate programs in biomedical engineering means that there will be an increased number of biomedical engineers to fill those positions.

The rise in biomedical engineering jobs is attributed to an aging population and increasing demand for improved medical devices and systems. Specific areas of growth are expected to be in computer-assisted surgery, cellular and tissue engineering, rehabilitation, and orthopedic engineering.

EARNINGS

The U.S. Bureau of Labor Statistics reported that the median income for biomedical engineers was $57,480 in 2000, with the lowest 10 percent earning less than $36,860 and the highest 10 percent earning more than $90,000. The 2001 salary survey of the National Association of Colleges and Employers reported average starting salary offers of $47,850 for bachelor's-degree candidates in biomedical engineering and $62,600 for master's-degree candidates.

ADDITIONAL SOURCES OF INFORMATION

American Medical Informatics Association
4915 St. Elmo Avenue, Suite 401
Bethesda, MD 20814
amia.org

American Society for Healthcare Engineering (ASHE)
One North Franklin, Twenty-Seventh Floor
Chicago, IL 60606
ashe.org

Biomedical Engineering Society (BMES)
8401 Corporate Drive, Suite 110
Landover, MD 20785-2224
bmes.org

Society of Biomedical Equipment Technicians
3330 Washington Boulevard, Fourth Floor
Arlington, VA 22201

The Whitaker Foundation
1700 North Moore Street, Suite 2200
Rosslyn, VA 22209
whitaker.org

CHAPTER

16

COMPUTER ENGINEERING

Computers are in every aspect of our lives today! Everything from car engines, microwave ovens, video games, watches, cell phones, pagers, and laptop computers to household appliances relies on computers. Thanks to the advances of computer engineers, it is possible to produce high-quality, high-tech products for everyday use as well as for complex scientific use. Despite the problems of the dot-com and telecommunications industry in 2000, the computer industry still remains one of the most important segments of our economy.

Therefore, computer engineering, although traditionally a part of electrical and electronics engineering, has begun to be recognized as a separate engineering entity. It can either be studied as a specialty area within electrical engineering or it can be pursued as a college major in its own right at institutions that offer a degree specifically in computer engineering. Computer engineering crosses the boundaries of many engineering disciplines and depends on the talents and services of other engineers in developing and implementing computer systems. This is particularly true in the case of specialized computer systems, such as those designed for agricultural, biomedical, chemical, transportation, or automotive purposes.

THE NATURE OF THE WORK

The opportunities in computer engineering cross the dividing lines of other engineering disciplines because the production of computers requires collaboration by many engineering specialists. When compared to most other engineering groups, computer engineers tend to perform more of their work in teams. In this collaboration, it is computer engineers who analyze solutions, design, develop, manufacture, install, and test computer equipment and software, utilizing advanced communications or multimedia equipment.

In the field of computer engineering, there are three major types of engineers: computer hardware engineers, computer systems engineers (including both software and network engineers), and computer information science engineers.

Computer Hardware Engineers

Computer hardware engineers, or electronics engineers, research, design, develop, and test computer hardware. They also supervise the manufacture and installation of computer chips, circuit boards, computer systems, keyboards, modems, and printers.

Computer Systems Engineers

Computer systems engineers determine what the computer is to do and how it is to perform tasks. This category of engineer tends to be divided into two groups. The first group is *software engineers*. These engineers design and develop software systems that combine the particular characteristics of the computer hardware with its software applications (programs) and/or operating systems. Their work enables the computer chips to function in a unified manner and produce a desired result.

The second group is *network engineers*. These engineers install and manage computer hubs, switches, routers, and firewalls, as well as IT (information technology) server structures running products such as Netware, Windows NT, Linux, and Unix. They assure that all systems are running smoothly, and they take care of problems and plan new IT projects.

Computer Information Science Engineers

Computer information science engineers determine the manner in which the computer can best serve the user. They design databases to store and retrieve even the most minute bits of information on a multitude of subjects. Computer information science engineers emphasize the arrangement of input and output data rather than the mechanics of computing.

According to IEEE, some of the areas in which computer engineers work are as follows:

- *Artificial intelligence.* Developing computers that simulate human learning and reasoning ability.
- *Computer design and engineering.* Designing new computer circuits, microchips, and other electronic components.
- *Computer architecture.* Designing new computer instruction sets and combining electronic or optical components to provide powerful but cost-effective computing.
- *Information technology.* Developing and managing information systems that support a business or organization. "IT embodies the hardware, software, algorithms, databases, tactics, and man-machine interfaces used to create, capture, organize, modify, store, protect, access, and distribute information for ultimate use by people," according to the Task Force on Information Technology for Business Applications.
- *Software engineering.* Developing methods for the production of software systems on time, within budget, and with few or no defects.
- *Computer theory.* Investigating the fundamental theories of how computers solve problems, and applying the results to other areas of computer science.
- *Operating systems and networks.* Developing the basic software computers use to supervise themselves or to communicate with other computers.
- *Software applications.* Applying computer science and technology to solving problems outside the computer field—in education or medicine, for example.

THE SETTINGS IN WHICH COMPUTER ENGINEERS WORK

Computer professionals work in almost every environment including academia, research, industry, government, private, and business organizations. However, computer hardware and computer systems engineers tend to work in different settings.

According to the U.S. Bureau of Labor Statistics, computer hardware engineers held about sixty thousand jobs in 2000. About 25 percent were employed in computer and data processing services. About one out of ten worked in computer and office equipment manufacturing, but many also are employed in communications industries and engineering consulting firms.

By contrast, the U.S. Bureau of Labor Statistics found that computer software engineers held about 697,000 jobs in 2000. Almost 46 percent of these engineers are employed in the computer and data processing services industry, which develops and produces prepackaged software as well as provides programming, systems integration, and information retrieval, including online databases and Internet services on a contract basis.

In addition, all types of computer engineers work for government agencies, manufacturers of computers and related electronic equipment, colleges and universities, and a wide range of industries. Those who work in industry are employed in all types and sizes of organizations, from start-up companies to large, established corporations.

EDUCATION AND OTHER QUALIFICATIONS

Because computer engineering is considered a part of the electrical and electronics engineering field, computer engineers will take the same general core courses as electrical engineers. In the junior and senior years, however, the degree and amount of specialization will vary according to a student's chosen track.

The following curricula show the typical courses required for electrical and computer engineering and for computer science and engineering:

Electrical and Computer Engineering
Math
Physics and chemistry

Introductory computing

Mechanics and thermodynamics

Electromagnetic fields

Logic circuits and lab

Computer architecture and switching

Circuits and electronics and labs

Energy conversion

Linear systems

Oral/written communications

Social science/humanities

Computer Science and Engineering

Math

Physics or chemistry

Introductory computing

Computer hardware and microcomputers

Software engineering

Lab and design work

Engineering

Computer science and engineering electives

Oral/written communications

Social science/humanities

Computer science and engineering programs generally have fewer courses in physics or chemistry. Instead of mechanics, thermodynamics, and energy conversion courses, the curriculum contains more electives in numerical methods, database design, operating systems, and artificial intelligence.

Four-year undergraduate computing programs are accredited by either the Computing Sciences Accreditation Board (CSAB) or the Accreditation Board for Engineering and Technology (ABET).

OUTLOOK FOR THE FUTURE

Because computers are now used to control devices such as the space shuttle, medical devices, and household appliances, the demand for all types of computer engineers will not only continue, it is expected to increase through the end of this decade. The greatest need will be for those involved in designing, developing, managing, upgrading, and customizing increasingly complex systems. In addition, computer engineers who specialize in embedded systems will find themselves in increasing demand.

Employment opportunities for computer engineers will not only exist in the computer and office equipment industry, but in industries that are increasingly relying on computer applications. These industries include the medical, automotive, security, and transportation industries. Consulting firms will also provide increased opportunities for computer engineers. While computer engineering is a relatively young field, vacancies will also result from the need to replace retired workers as well as those who change career fields or leave the labor force.

EARNINGS

In 2001, the average starting salary for bachelor's-degree graduates in computer engineering was $53,924 a year; for master's-degree candidates it was $58,026 a year; and for Ph.D. candidates it was $70,140, according to the National Association of Colleges and Employers. Likewise, the U.S. Bureau of Labor Statistics reported median annual earnings in the following fields:

Computer and office equipment $75,730
Computer and data processing services $69,490
Electronic components and accessories $67,800
Telephone communication $59,160

These industries employed the largest numbers of computer engineers. When looking at the field at large, the median annual earnings were $67,300 in 2000.

ADDITIONAL SOURCES OF INFORMATION

Accreditation Board for Engineering and Technology (ABET)
111 Market Place, Suite 1050
Baltimore, MD 21202
abet.org

American Electronics Association (AEA)
5201 Great American Parkway, Suite 520
P.O. Box 54990
Santa Clara, CA 95054
aeanet.org

American Society for Information Science and Technology
1320 Fenwick Lane, Suite 510
Silver Spring, MD 20910
asis.org

Association for Computing Machinery
1515 Broadway
New York, NY 10036
acm.org

Association for Women in Computing (AWC)
41 Sutter Street, Suite 1006
San Francisco, CA 94104
awc-hq.org

Computer Science Accreditation Board, Inc. (CSAB)
184 North Street
Stamford, CT 06901
csab.org

Computer Science Accreditation Commission
111 Market Place, Suite 1050
Baltimore, MD 21202
csab.org/acrsch.html

IEEE Computer Society Offices
1730 Massachusetts Avenue NW
Washington, DC 20036-1992
computer.org/contact.htm

Information Handling Services (IHS)
6160 South Syracuse Way
Englewood, CO 80150
ihs.com

Robotic Industries Association (RIA)
900 Victors Way
P.O. Box 3724
Ann Arbor, MI 48106
robotics.org

C H A P T E R

ENVIRONMENTAL ENGINEERING

Environmental engineering can trace its history back to the 1800s and to the field of sanitation engineering. Today environmental engineers play a vital role in working to reduce the pollution and toxicants in our air, water, and ground in order to preserve a better quality of life for all living things. In order to enter this field, it is possible to study a specialty area in chemical or civil engineering or pursue a degree in environmental engineering in its own right at institutions that offer more in-depth preparation specifically in environmental engineering. Regardless of which educational path is chosen, environmental engineers have limitless opportunities in the type of work that they do.

THE NATURE OF THE WORK

Environmental engineers use the principles of biology, chemistry, and engineering to develop methods of solving problems related to the environment. The American Academy of Environmental Engineers states that engineers in this field work in a wide variety of areas, and each area has a number of subcategories. The areas in which environmental engineers tend to work are:

Air pollution control
Industrial hygiene

Radiation protection

Hazardous waste management

Recycling

Toxic materials control

Water supply

Wastewater management

Storm water management

Solid waste disposal

Public health

Land management

According to the U.S. Department of Labor, "Environmental engineers conduct hazardous-waste management studies, evaluate the significance of the hazard, offer analysis on treatment and containment, and develop regulations to prevent mishaps. They design municipal sewage and industrial wastewater systems. They analyze scientific data, research controversial projects, and perform quality control checks. . . . They study and attempt to minimize the effects of acid rain, global warming, automobile emissions, and ozone depletion. They also are involved in the protection of wildlife. . . . They help clients comply with regulations and clean up hazardous sites, including brownfields, which are abandoned urban or industrial sites that may contain environmental hazards."

Environmental engineers work in many capacities. They are researchers, designers, planners, operators of pollution-control facilities, professors, government regulatory agency officials, and managers of programs.

THE SETTINGS IN WHICH ENVIRONMENTAL ENGINEERS WORK

In 2000, the U.S Bureau of Labor Statistics reported that environmental engineers held about fifty-two thousand jobs. These positions are divided fairly evenly among various manufacturing industries; federal, state, and local government agencies; and engineering and management consulting firms. In addition, environmental engineers are employed by universities and by research firms and testing laboratories.

Increasingly there are international opportunities for environmental engineers. Many of these positions exist in Eastern Europe. And, because there is a strong relationship between pollution and population, many opportunities for environmental engineers exist in urban areas with large concentrations of people.

EDUCATION AND OTHER QUALIFICATIONS

Like biomedical engineering, it is recommended that high school students prepare for the study of environmental engineering by taking the same courses recommended for any other engineering discipline (algebra, geometry, calculus, trigonometry, physics, and chemistry). However, for those interested in environmental engineering it is also expected that life science courses will be included. Advanced placement (AP) courses in math and science would also be strongly suggested.

The American Academy of Environmental Engineers states that entry-level positions in environmental engineering require a B.S. in engineering. The degree can be in civil, chemical, mechanical, or environmental engineering. In addition to college courses in math, science, engineering mechanics, humanities, writing, and speaking, students interested in environmental engineering will take courses such as organic chemistry, computational modeling, fluid mechanics, hydraulic engineering, and engineering graphics. They may also take courses such as environmental engineering systems, environmental impact evaluation, public health engineering, community air pollution, sanitary engineering, ecosystems and ecotoxicology, aquatic chemistry, or environmental engineering design.

In the field of environmental engineering, a master's degree or a Ph.D. are strongly recommended. However, advanced degrees are no substitute for experience. Therefore, during the undergraduate program it is advisable to participate in cooperative engineering education (co-op), or at least summer internships. In some states, co-op experience may count toward the experience needed to sit for the second exam in the Professional Engineering (P.E.) license process.

OUTLOOK FOR THE FUTURE

According to both the American Academy of Environmental Engineers and the National Science Foundation, there have never been enough environmental engineers. Now that worldwide environmental problems have grown more complex, the demand for environmental engineers continues to grow. In fact, through 2010, the U.S. Labor Department expects the employment of environmental engineers to increase.

Environmental engineers will not only be needed to meet new environmental regulations but to develop methods of cleaning up existing hazards. In recent years there has been a shift in the approach to environmental issues. Now it is preferable that environmental problems be prevented rather than trying to control or clean up problems that already exist. It is projected that this new emphasis will also increase the demand for environmental engineers. Political factors such as this significantly impact the job outlook for environmental engineers. When federal, state, or local legislation reduces funding to enforce environmental regulations, job opportunities decrease. Likewise, when funding is increased to enforce new or existing environmental regulations, opportunities also increase.

Compared to most other types of engineers, environmental engineers are more likely to be impacted by political factors and by significant economic downturns. During these downturns, there tends to be less emphasis on environmental protection issues. Therefore, it is important that environmental engineers stay abreast of political and economic issues as well as environmental issues.

EARNINGS

As the 1990s drew to a close, the American Academy of Environmental Engineers reported that bachelor's-degree engineers received starting salary offers ranging from $36,000 to $42,000 annually. However, by 2001, the National Association of Colleges and Employers reported that bachelor's-degree candidates in environmental engineering received starting offers averaging $51,167 a year.

Environmental engineers with five years' experience or more who obtain the P.E. license can expect to earn well above $60,000 to $65,000. The U.S. Bureau of Labor Statistics reported that the median annual earnings of environmental engineers were $57,780 in 2000, with the lowest 10 percent earning less than $37,210 and the highest 10 percent earning more than $87,290.

ADDITIONAL SOURCES OF INFORMATION

Air and Waste Management Association (AWMA)
One Gateway Center, Third Floor
Pittsburgh, PA 15222
awma.org

Alliance to Save Energy (ASE)
1200 Eighteenth Street NW, Suite 90
Washington, DC 20036
ase.org

American Academy of Environmental Engineers
130 Holiday Court, Suite 100
Annapolis, MD 21401
aaee.net

American Council of Engineering Companies
Environmental Business Action Coalition (EBAC)
1015 Fifteenth Street NW
Washington, DC 20005
acec.org

American Industrial Hygiene Association (AIHA)
2700 Prosperity Avenue, Suite 250
Fairfax, VA 22031
aiha.org

American Institute of Chemical Engineers (AICHE)
Three Park Avenue
New York, NY 10016-5991
aiche.org

American Society of Civil Engineers (ASCE)
1801 Alexander Bell Drive
Reston, VA 20191-4400
asce.org
ASCE Institute (asce.org/inst_found):
Environmental and Water Resources Institute (EWRI)

American Society of Mechanical Engineers (ASME)
Three Park Avenue
New York, NY 10016
asme.org

American Society of Safety Engineers (ASSE)
1800 East Oakton Street
Des Plaines, IL 60018
asse.org

American Society of Sanitary Engineering, Inc. (ASSE)
28901 Clemens Road, Suite 100
Westlake, OH 44145
asse-plumbing.org

American Water Works Association (AWWA)
6666 West Quincy
Denver, CO 80235
awwa.org

Institute of Professional Environmental Practice (IPEP)
600 Forbes Avenue
333 Fisher Hall
Pittsburgh, PA 15282
ipep.org

National Council of Examiners for Engineering and Surveying
P.O. Box 1686
Clemson, SC 29633-1686
ncees.org

National Council on Radiation Protection and Measurements (NCRP)
7910 Woodmont Avenue, Suite 800
Bethesda, MD 20814
ncrp.com

Portland Cement Association (PCA)
5420 Old Orchard Road
Skokie, IL 60077-1083
portcement.org

Solid Waste Association of North America
1100 Wayne Avenue
Silver Spring, MD 20910
swana.org

Water Environment Federation
601 Wythe Street
Alexandria, VA 22314-1994
wef.org

C H A P T E R
18

MANUFACTURING ENGINEERING

Manufacturing is a wealth-creating profession. The federal government has always recognized this fact, but in the 1990s it formed the Manufacturing Engineering Laboratory (MEL) to contribute to improvements in the capabilities and performance of virtually every phase of manufacturing in this country. As a result of this commitment of research and funds, U.S. manufacturing has become more and more high-tech.

Today's manufacturing facilities are no longer the old smokestack and dirt assembly line places that dominated the twentieth century. They now involve robotic devices, computer-integrated systems, E-commerce, green manufacturing, and other new technologies, making them dynamic and innovative places to work. A tour of a modern manufacturing facility is like a trip into a futuristic space and time. As a result, there is an increasing need for engineers who are trained for this work environment. It is not necessary to specifically major in manufacturing engineering to enter this field. Manufacturing engineers can pursue a specialty in such traditional majors as industrial, mechanical, electrical, or chemical engineering. However, in recent years more schools of engineering have added manufacturing engineering as a major in its own right. This phenomenon reflects the increased demand by manufacturers for engineers who are highly educated for the field. Manufacturing engineers not only like to make things, but they like to make them better, faster, and at a lower cost. They want to be involved from the initial design process to final production. These are the people who enjoy working with other people, as part of a team or as the team's leader.

THE NATURE OF THE WORK

Manufacturing engineers apply manufacturing sciences and technology to improve production. They utilize fundamental engineering skills based in mathematics, science, and the scientific method as well as contemporary tools and techniques to identify and solve manufacturing and service industry problems. They understand, analyze, and design industrial and service processes, systems, and work environments.

Manufacturing engineers deal with all aspects of the production processes. They are the engineers concerned with the design and operation of integrated systems that produce high-quality, affordable products that utilize computer networks, robots, machine tools, and high-tech materials-handling equipment. In order to do so, manufacturing engineers take an interdisciplinary approach to their work.

Manufacturing engineers can specialize in a variety of specific technologies. Some of these specialties include designing "smart" materials, controlling chemical and other manufacturing processes, and expanding the use of microelectronics and manufacturing microsystems. In fact, some collegiate programs combine the study of manufacturing engineering with other technology areas so that graduates are prepared to work in specific manufacturing industries. An example of this type of program might be an aerospace manufacturing program that prepares students for positions with manufacturers of small aircraft, jetliners, or spacecraft.

Manufacturing engineers assure that their solutions are economically viable and meet industrial health, safety, and all other relevant legislation. They cover the entire field of manufacturing engineering including machine tools, materials processing, sensors and controllers, computer-integrated manufacturing and robotics, and manufacturing systems management and optimization. That is why the Society of Manufacturing Engineers (SME) has eleven different manufacturing-related categories to which its fifty thousand members can choose to belong. They are:

Automation and integration
Composites manufacturing
Electronic manufacturing
Finishing processes
Machine vision
Machining
Manufacturing research
Material forming and fabricating
Plastics
Robotics
Rapid prototyping

The categories demonstrate the range of modern issues that face manufacturing industries. As a result, manufacturing engineers have responsibility for a wide variety of tasks, including such things as:

- Automating manufacturing facilities using computer-integrated technology
- Improving productivity by analyzing operations
- Developing scheduling systems
- Developing assignments for machines and equipment
- Implementing quality-control programs
- Identifying cost-effective material handling and facility layout alternatives
- Designing management information systems
- Designing operator workstations—including seating, work surfaces, displays, and controls

THE SETTINGS IN WHICH MANUFACTURING ENGINEERS WORK

There is really no limit to where manufacturing engineers can work. Choices are not limited to certain industries. These engineers are needed wherever products are manufactured. They are not limited by location because manufacturing is carried out around the world. In addition, manufacturing environments allow for a variety of experiences, which keep the work challenging and interesting. The *Dictionary of Occupational Titles* provides a comprehensive breakdown of sixty-two businesses and industries in which engineers are employed, ranging from abrasive and polishing industries to wood distillation industries and everything in between.

Service industries, such as health-care management and transportation, also provide opportunities for manufacturing engineers.

EDUCATION AND OTHER QUALIFICATIONS

Manufacturing engineering requires well-educated graduates because of the complexity of the work. In order to enroll in a collegiate manufacturing engineering curriculum, high school students should have at least two years of high school algebra and one year of trigonometry and physics. High school chemistry and calculus are also recommended.

The first two years of the college curriculum include fundamental courses in physics, chemistry, math, and engineering. Depending on the emphasis of the program at a particular college or university, courses in the last two years not only focus on advanced content in engineering and manufacturing but can include human-machine systems engineering; geographical information systems for engineering applications; advanced manufacturing processes; design for manufacture; electronic commerce; engineering products; engineering management; engineering data management; improving performance and quality; composite materials in mechanical systems; ISO 14000 international standards; microelectromechanical systems (MEMS); accident and liability risks; robust engineering; geometric tolerancing; project management; finance and accounting for project management; fundamentals of inventory management and control; and communications skills for managers.

Most manufacturing engineering programs have a strong "practice-based" component. Some require structured internships, and others may take five years to complete because of the hands-on experience that students are required to obtain. Many manufacturing engineering programs either urge or require students to participate in cooperative engineering education (co-op). Gaining industrial experience to complement academic studies is highly regarded by the industries that seek manufacturing engineers after graduation.

Once in the field, manufacturing engineers can obtain professional certification from the Society of Manufacturing Engineers (SME) in one of three categories:

- Certified Manufacturing Technologist (C.Mfg.T.)
- Certified Manufacturing Engineer (C.Mfg.E.)
- Certified Enterprise Integrator (C.E.I.)

Manufacturing engineers can also obtain the Professional Engineering (P.E.) license, which is highly recommended for those engineers working for companies with international facilities. After gaining several years of experience, many manufacturing engineers combine their technical expertise with their business experience to pursue an M.B.A.

OUTLOOK FOR THE FUTURE

Because of the importance of the manufacturing sector to the U.S. economy, and the important role that manufacturing engineers play in improving manufacturing efficiency and productivity, the employment outlook for manufacturing engineers is quite favorable. In the new era of global and decentralized manufacturing, the skills of the manufacturing engineer are in increasing demand.

EARNINGS

Beginning salaries for manufacturing engineering graduates range from $44,000 to $55,000, with those of graduates of master's-degree programs in manufacturing engineering being higher. However, the salaries for manufacturing engineers are most closely tied to the type of industry in which they work. For example, manufacturing engineers in the chemical industries should look at salary information for chemical engineers. Likewise, manufacturing engineers in the computer or aerospace industries will want to consider salary information for aerospace, electrical, or computer engineers. Otherwise it is recommended that the salaries of industrial or mechanical engineers be used as a guide.

ADDITIONAL SOURCES OF INFORMATION

American Architectural Manufacturers Association (AAMA)
1827 Walden Office Square, Suite 104
Schaumburg, IL 60173
aamanet.org

American Boiler Manufacturers Association (ABMA)
950 North Glebe Road, Suite 160
Arlington, VA 22203
abma.com

American Society of Mechanical Engineers (ASME)
Three Park Avenue
New York, NY 10016
asme.org

Association for Facilities Engineers (AFE)
Formerly the American Institute of Plant Engineers (AIPE)
8180 Corporate Park Drive, Suite 305
Cincinnati, OH 45242
afe.org

Institute of Electrical and Electronics Engineers, Inc. (IEEE)
Three Park Avenue, Seventeenth Floor
New York, NY 10016-5997
ieee.org
IEEE society offices:
IEEE Components, Packaging, and Manufacturing
Technology Society

Manufacturing Engineering Laboratory (MEL)
B322 Metrology Building
100 Bureau Drive, Stop 8200
Gaithersburg, MD 20899-8200
mel.nist.gov

National Electrical Manufacturers Association (NEMA)
1300 North Seventeenth Street, Suite 1847
Rosslyn, VA 22209
nema.org

National Electrical Manufacturers Representatives Association
   (NEMRA)
200 Business Park Drive, Suite 301
Armonk, NY 10504
nemra.org

Society of Manufacturing Engineers (SME)
One SME Drive
P.O. Box 930
Dearborn, MI 48121-0930
sme.org

CHAPTER

19

PETROLEUM ENGINEERING*

Petroleum engineers are involved in searching for petroleum, commonly referred to as oil, and natural gas reserves and the recovery of these natural resources for use by society. The work in the industry continues to expand in scope to address the increased importance placed on environmental concerns as well as the implementation of new technologies that allow for more efficient and thorough retrieval of oil and natural gas. People who wish to enter the petroleum engineering field can either pursue a degree in chemical, civil, environmental, mechanical, or electrical engineering or they can pursue a degree in petroleum engineering in its own right at institutions that offer more in-depth preparation for the field.

Oil and natural gas provide approximately three-fifths of our energy needs. The oil and natural gas fuels homes, workplaces, factories, and transportation as well as being the raw material from which plastics, chemicals, medicines, fertilizers, and synthetic fibers are made. Oil and natural gas, formed by the decomposition of plants and animals deep underground, under tremendous heat and pressure for millions of years, are fundamental to modern society and will continue to be important well into the future even as efforts intensify to reduce dependence on fossil fuels.

---

*Content contributed by John Fabijanic.

THE NATURE OF THE WORK

Petroleum engineers can take on many different responsibilities in the exploration for and retrieval of oil and natural gas. The overall responsibility of a petroleum engineer is to develop and implement the most cost-effective and efficient recovery of oil and natural gas. Major areas of responsibility include, but are not limited to, the following:

Drilling Engineer

The drilling engineer designs the drilling apparatus and support operations to extract the fossil fuel. Drilling engineers work closely with geologists and other specialists to understand the geology and rock formations of the reservoir. These operations are often multimillion-dollar investments in time and resources.

Production Engineer

The production engineer develops processes to retrieve the oil and natural gas in an efficient and cost-effective manner using techniques such as water, steam, gas, and chemical injection, computer-controlled drilling, and fracturing.

Reservoir Engineer

Reservoir engineers perform analyses to determine important parameters such as ideal recovery pressures. Reservoir engineers regularly use sophisticated computer models for simulating the petroleum reserve and the performance of different techniques of recovery. Much of the work involves the determination of cost-benefit analysis for the recovery effort justified for each petroleum discovery.

Research and Development and Environmental Engineers

Even with modern techniques like water, steam, gas, and chemical injection, computer-controlled drilling, and fracturing to connect multiple reservoirs, only a small amount of the oil in a reservoir can be retrieved.

Petroleum engineers are also involved in the research and development of new technology to more completely recover and lower the cost of retrieval of fossil fuels.

Petroleum engineers specializing in environmental engineering are becoming increasingly important as environmental regulations and public demand for environmental protection become more prevalent.

THE SETTINGS IN WHICH PETROLEUM ENGINEERS WORK

Petroleum engineers are found predominantly in oil and gas extraction, refining, and engineering and architectural services. Consulting firms and government agencies also employ petroleum engineers. In the United States the great majority of petroleum engineers work for larger companies that employ fifty or more workers. However, over 70 percent of companies involved in the petroleum industry employ fewer than ten people. The greatest concentrations of opportunities for petroleum engineers are found in Louisiana, Oklahoma, California, and Texas.

The search for and retrieval of fossil fuels occurs worldwide and can often result in the petroleum engineer working in exotic locations like remote jungles, deserts, or mountain ranges. Those willing to work on assignments or be based overseas will find many opportunities in the petroleum industry.

For most petroleum engineers work time is split between the office and field operations. The exact split of time is defined by the engineer's responsibilities and the scope of the project. Engineers working primarily at field locations often work nonstandard workweeks and hours, although the extra days or hours are generally well compensated. Positions consisting of primarily office-based work are not uncommon. Still other positions are on offshore rigs far from shore. In these locations, petroleum engineers may spend long periods at sea and live on a support ship.

EDUCATION AND OTHER QUALIFICATIONS

The Society of Petroleum Engineers encourages those who wish to pursue a career in petroleum engineering to take courses in earth science, chemistry, physics, algebra, trigonometry, and calculus. The petroleum industry is multinational in its scope, and the study of foreign languages is also recommended.

A petroleum engineer will need a minimum of a bachelor's degree, although many companies prefer to hire candidates with a master's degree. Research positions often require a Ph.D. Those with degrees in chemical, civil, and mechanical engineering are also often considered for petroleum engineering positions. The college curriculum for a bachelor's degree begins with a focus on mastering the fundamentals of math, science, and engineering. Specialized courses leading to a petroleum engineering degree include courses in geology, formation evaluation, drilling, reservoir properties, and production.

OUTLOOK FOR THE FUTURE

According to the Bureau of Labor Statistics, the employment of petroleum engineers is expected to decline through 2010, largely because most of the petroleum-production areas in the United States have been explored. Additionally, strict regulation and limited access to public lands has limited both land and offshore exploration in the United States. The limitation of opportunities for exploration and drilling in the United States leads the petroleum companies to pursue more lucrative foreign locations. This situation may change if the regulations concerning exploration and drilling on public lands are changed. Worldwide investment in the petroleum industry is also subject to the varying market price for petroleum and natural gas. However, worldwide demand for petroleum products is expected to grow, and some within the industry see a significantly brighter future for the petroleum industry as it expands into the general energy market and works to meet worldwide demand amid tougher and more stringent regulations.

In spite of the projected decline, according to the Bureau of Labor Statistics, in total employment of petroleum engineers, the need to replace petroleum engineers who transfer to other occupations or leave the workforce will exceed the relatively small number of graduates. Therefore, the outlook for employment of petroleum engineering graduates is good.

Petroleum engineers work throughout the world, and those who are willing to work abroad and/or who speak one or more foreign languages will be in particular demand. U.S.-trained petroleum engineers are in demand with many foreign employers, and the best employment opportunities may be overseas, especially as the petroleum engineer gains more experience.

EARNINGS

Petroleum engineers enjoy some of the highest starting salaries of any engineering field. According to a 2001 salary survey by the National Association of Colleges and Employers, the average annual starting salary was $53,880 for a person with a bachelor's degree in petroleum engineering. For the graduate with a master's degree in petroleum engineering the average starting salary was $58,500 per year.

From the Bureau of Labor Statistics, the median income of petroleum engineers was $78,910 in 2000, with the middle 50 percent earning between $60,610 and $100,210.

ADDITIONAL SOURCES OF INFORMATION

American Institute of Chemical Engineers (AICHE)
Three Park Avenue
New York, NY 10016-5991
aiche.org

Society of Petroleum Engineering
P.O. Box 833836
Richardson, TX 75083-3836
spe.org

American Petroleum Institute
1220 L Street NW
Washington, DC 20005-4070
api.org

C H A P T E R

ENGINEERING TECHNOLOGY*

Engineering technology constitutes a wide range of skills and methods. Engineering technologists work closely with engineers. They assist engineers in planning and implementing their designs and inventions. To understand what engineering technology is, let's take a closer look at the difference between the engineer and the engineering technologist.

In their jobs, technologists and engineers often perform similar tasks; however, the engineer is more often concerned with developing the overall plans and designs, while the technologist is more concerned with the implementation or completion of a specific part of a plan or design. Put another way, the engineer is concerned with the application of scientific knowledge or "why" something is to be done. The engineering technologist is concerned with the actual performance and completion of the application developed by the engineer, or the "what" needs to be done to achieve what the engineer has designed or specified.

As an example, a chemical engineer will know why two specific compounds when mixed will yield the desired results in a scientifically rigorous manner. The engineering technician will know what needs to be done to safely and efficiently produce and mix the compounds specified by the chemical engineer. The engineer's and technologist's areas of experience

---

*Content contributed by John Fabijanic.

often overlap, and both are vital in the process of taking an abstract idea or goal to a successful reality.

The American Society for Engineering Education has defined engineering technology in the following way:

> Engineering technology is that part of the technological field which requires the application of scientific and engineering knowledge and methods combined with technical skills in support of engineering activities; it lies in the area between the craftsman and the engineer in the part closest to the engineer.

The technologist is concerned with achieving practical objectives through the application of procedures, methods, and techniques that have been proved by experience over the years. In developing plans and designs to solve complex problems, the engineer cannot develop a single, obvious best answer or plan. In solving technical problems that are sections or subsets of a large engineering plan or design, the technologist may be able to achieve a unique or specific solution.

The engineer must consider many nontechnical factors in developing plans and designs, including legal restraints, social impacts, economic factors, and aesthetic considerations. In solving technical problems, the technologist generally is not faced with such constraints and is usually able to concentrate on the physical and economic factors of the problem.

The engineer must exercise judgment in solving many problems to obtain the optimum benefit for society. In general, engineering technologists are not called upon to make such complex judgments, but they often must estimate and approximate conditions that cannot be completely known.

TECHNOLOGY SPECIALISTS

With the tremendous growth in technology and the increasing complexity of the applications of scientific and empirical technology, it has become increasingly necessary for technologists to specialize in one of the many distinct branches of engineering and technology. At the same time, there has arisen a separation in which certain people in a field concentrate on the development of designs and plans for the accomplishment of a given objective while another group of specialists concentrates on the practical application and implementation of those designs and plans. Hence, there is a need for both engineers and engineering technologists.

Finally, the individuals who are concerned with the practical applications—the technologists—have been divided into two classes, technicians and technologists. In general, these terms are used to designate persons with differing levels of education or experience in their field. The term *engineering technician* is applied to a person who has graduated from a two-year technology curriculum and has obtained an associate degree in applied science or engineering technology. The term *technologist* usually is reserved for the graduate of a four-year bachelor of engineering technology program or for the technician who has gained wide experience in the field through many years of practice in engineering technology.

The field of engineering technology covers a broad spectrum of activities, and the engineering technologist specializes in one branch of engineering or another. In this section we will take a look at the four main branches of engineering technology—civil engineering technology, mechanical engineering technology, electrical engineering technology, and chemical engineering technology.

Civil Engineering Technology

The most prominent activity in the civil engineering field is structural design. Technologists involved in this activity are concerned with some phase of the design of buildings, dams, and bridges. Structures must be designed and constructed to withstand their own weight as well as such natural forces as earthquakes and winds, and they must be suited to the environments in which they are built. The need to accommodate extremes in climatic and environmental conditions constantly presents new problems and challenges to the engineering team that is concerned with structural design and construction.

Civil engineering technologists often are employed directly in supervising and monitoring the construction of various facilities. In these activities, it is necessary to see that the structures under construction are built exactly according to the plans. Additionally, the technician and technologist often are charged with maintaining the quality of the materials used in construction. The engineering technologist working in construction also supervises the use of such heavy equipment as trucks, cranes, earthmovers, concrete mixing and placing equipment, and other devices and machines.

Another key occupational area of the civil engineering technologist is the construction and operation of transportation facilities such as highways, airports, and railroads. The technologist may be involved in the initial planning phases for such facilities, assisting the engineer in predicting the growth of population, the volume of anticipated traffic, potential future problems, and possible alternate locations for transportation facilities. In these studies, the technologist will be called upon to give full attention to the environmental impact of the construction and operation of transportation facilities.

As in other fields where the construction of facilities is a necessary and important activity, in transportation engineering the technologist is involved in constructing facilities efficiently under varying conditions of terrain and climate. He or she will be involved in surveying and mapping and in the supervision of construction. Finally, he or she also may be involved in the analysis of transportation systems to ensure the maximum efficiency of completed networks.

One of the oldest and most important areas of interest for civil engineers and technologists is that of hydraulics—otherwise known as the management of water resources. Included in this area are the collection, control, use, and conservation of water. Projects for flood control, drainage, reclamation, and irrigation are planned and designed by civil engineers and technologists who are specialists in hydraulics, as are navigation projects, water storage projects, and hydroelectric power plants.

One of the most important areas of activity for civil engineering technologists specializing in hydraulics is their work in assuring safe drinking water and effective sewage and wastewater disposal systems. With populations becoming more concentrated and modern industry growing rapidly, the amounts and kinds of pollutants poured into rivers and streams and other areas of the environment assure that engineers and technologists working in the area of water supply and wastewater treatment will find new challenges of ever-greater complexity.

In recent years, there has been a population shift from the country to the city. Civil engineering technologists working in construction, in structural design, in transportation, and in water management are concentrating many of their activities in population centers, solving the problems caused by this redistribution of people. Some civil engineering technologists devote their time primarily to working with city planners and urban development agencies, assisting them in formulating plans for growth and the management of urban areas.

Mechanical Engineering Technology

As the name indicates, the mechanical engineering technologist quite often is concerned with the development of machines. Mechanical engineering technicians are found in the many steps in the process of taking an idea or goal and efficiently producing a useful end product.

In the initial research and development, mechanical engineering technicians will aid the design, manufacture, assembly, and testing of research equipment or prototypes. The technician may use machine tools such as lathes, mills, grinders, and shapers to produce components. Alternatively, the technician may do all of the drafting and commands on a computer that will then control a lathe or mill. The mechanical engineering technician will often be responsible for the layout of equipment, setting up of test articles and test equipment, conducting tests, and writing reports.

As the project advances to preparation for production, mechanical engineering technicians will, in addition to the duties performed during the prototype phase, be involved in production planning, determination of the assembly process, and machinery requirements for the parts to be manufactured in the most efficient and cost-effective manner possible. Some technicians will inspect the equipment and monitor the production process for problems and suggest ways to improve the efficiency or reduce the occurrence of problems.

The mechanical engineering technician can perform some or all of these duties in as broad a range of endeavors as mechanical engineers are involved in. From the smallest plastic toy to the largest of airplanes or most complex of nuclear power plants, all have large mechanical engineering components that require mechanical engineering technicians to make things a reality. For example, mechanical engineers and technologists are deeply involved in the development of new power plants and mechanical configurations for automobiles and trucks. Because of the increasing scarcity of cheap petroleum fuels, great attention is being given to development of more economical engines and power plants for vehicles. Mechanical engineering technologists are employed to assist in the design and perfection of automotive vehicles and in the supervision of vehicle construction. Additionally, many technologists in this field are employed in the search for means to reduce air and noise pollution associated with automobiles and trucks.

Some mechanical engineering technologists are involved in developing other means of transport, including rapid transit systems and space exploration systems. Technologists can find employment with the manufacturers of aircraft and space vehicles, as well as with industries that produce such forms of transportation as elevators, conveyors, monorails, and escalators.

Mechanical engineering technologists are also concerned with the development and operation of heating and ventilating systems, including solar energy systems.

Electrical Engineering Technology

A student who is interested in a career in electrical engineering technology may wish to consider working in the field of electrical power generation and transmission, on the use of electrical power in the development of communications systems, or on developing new and more efficient lighting systems.

Electrical and electronics engineering technicians make up nearly half of all engineering technicians. With the continuing growth and importance of electronics to all fields of engineering, the need for electrical engineering technologists will also continue to expand. Electrical and electronics engineering technicians are involved in every phase of the design, testing, and manufacturing of electrical and electronic equipment. The range of projects can extend from communications, radar, data acquisition and measurement, medical monitoring equipment, and electronics control to computers.

The development of communications technology as a distinct area within electrical engineering technology has been very rapid during the last fifty years and continues at a great pace. Telecommunications is wide ranging; it makes possible everything from a traditional phone call to the entire array of modern multimedia and wireless communication. The sequence of communications devices based upon electricity and electronics began with the telegraph and has continued through the telephone, the wireless set, the radio, motion pictures with sound, telephoto transmitters, and television. A revolution in capabilities and availability of new technologies in communication and media has occurred in recent years, and these devices have been developed and manufactured in greater complexity with more reliability and at lower costs with each succeeding year. Now we have at our fingertips access to phenomenal technologies such as satellite communication and location, worldwide instant communication of many forms, and much more to come at an ever-increasing rate. Electrical engineering technologists can participate in the development and testing of new communication devices as well as in supervision of the manufacture of already developed devices.

Electrical engineers are instrumental in the design and maintenance of electronics, computers, and electronic/computer-controlled systems. They design electronic data acquisition systems, electronic controls, and computer circuits, plan computer layouts, and formulate mathematical models of technical problems that can be solved by computers. These electrical and electronic systems may be for the operation, control, and measuring of the subject of experimentation or control the processes of the manufacture of finished goods by controlling the machines making parts, mixing ingredients, and transporting goods.

The electrical engineering technologist is almost certain to become involved in some way in the design, manufacture, or use of such devices if this area is of interest to him or her. The use of computers and electronic systems is now present in every engineering field from testing through production and into every corner of the media and communications industry. Computers and electronics are integral parts of all the devices of modern life including toys, cell phones, and any number of technologies on the horizon. Electrical and electronics technicians are required to design, test, and produce the current and future amazing array of electronic products for modern society.

Chemical Engineering Technology

Chemical engineering technologists are involved with the preparation, separation, and analysis of chemical substances. They often study the composition and changes in composition of natural and synthetic substances. In these activities, chemical engineering technologists rely heavily on a background in chemistry. However, their activities are not limited to the preparation and analysis of chemical substances. The chemical engineer, as opposed to the chemist, is concerned with the maximum utilization of raw materials when mass-producing substances via technology that controls chemical and physical processes. Technologists work with chemical engineers in the development of new products, the design of new processes, and the planning and operation of chemical plants. They may assist chemical engineers in the manufacture and analysis of such chemicals as salts, acids, or alkalis, all of which are used in great quantities in modern manufacturing processes.

Technologists in chemical engineering also may be involved in the refining of such natural materials as petroleum and rubber. Petroleum is utilized as a fuel in such forms as natural gas, gasoline, kerosene, and fuel oil. The chemical engineering technologist may be involved in the refining and purifying of petroleum fuels, as well as in the manufacture of chemicals from petroleum (petrochemicals). This is a growing field in which chemical engineering technologists are being employed in ever-greater numbers.

Another growing field in the chemical engineering industry is the synthesis of biochemicals, produced in nature by plants and animals. The chemical engineering technologist working in this area is interested in developing such chemicals in great quantity, at a reasonable cost, and with a high degree of purity. In other words, the technologist is employed in trying to reproduce, in full-scale manufacturing plants, the biochemical processes that occur in nature.

In all of the activities mentioned, the technologist is involved in the production of a given chemical substance through control of a chemical and physical process. Because of the importance of process control, many technologists also are employed in the study and perfection of basic chemical and physical processes. Within engineering plants, they assist in the control and perfection of chemical reactions. They are also concerned with the design of separation equipment and the development of control systems for the separation process.

One of the most important applications of separation combines the work of the chemical engineering technologist with that of the civil engineering technologist. These professionals collaborate in the use of separation operations to purify drinking water and to treat sewage waste. In utilizing such operations, chemical engineering technologists try to make reactions proceed as rapidly as possible with the lowest input of energy, to achieve the greatest efficiency and the lowest cost.

EDUCATION AND OTHER QUALIFICATIONS

Within the last twenty years, a new type of engineering technology program leading to a bachelor of technology degree has been established in institutes, colleges, and universities throughout the United States. These programs developed for a number of reasons, the most important of which appears to be the increasing complexity of modern technology. The applications of science in today's world have become so varied and complex that it is now necessary to acquire a high degree of specialization. Thus, many two-year engineering technology programs have been expanded into four-year programs that compare in technical content to the four-year engineering programs that existed in this country a generation ago.

Students can elect to earn a bachelor's degree in engineering or one in engineering technology. The baccalaureate engineering graduate very likely will hold a position in research, conceptual design, or systems engineering. The holder of a degree in engineering technology probably will be working in operations, product design, product development, or technical sales. The associate engineering technology graduate very likely will hold a position in support of an engineer's work.

A program leading to an engineering degree consists of courses in physical science, engineering science, and advanced mathematics through differential equations. The course of study leading to a bachelor's degree in engineering technology includes courses in technology, applied science, and mathematics through differential and integral calculus. The associate engineering technology program offers courses in science, skills, and mathematics through algebra.

We have seen, then, that at the present time two options in engineering technology education are open to high school graduates: the two-year associate degree program, to become an engineering technician; and the four-year bachelor of engineering technology program, which allows one to become an engineering technologist. These degrees are offered in several types of institutions, including the armed forces, technical institutes, community and junior colleges, and universities. Approximately 150 colleges offer programs leading to associate degrees in engineering technology, and nearly 100 colleges and universities offer programs leading to the bachelor of engineering technology degree. The quality and content of training programs vary widely, and training programs should be investigated closely including the kinds of jobs graduates obtain, the facilities, and the faculty qualifications. Additionally, it may be advisable to contact prospective employers regarding their preferences.

OUTLOOK FOR THE FUTURE

The employment opportunities for engineering technologists and technicians are subject to the same cyclical pressures as the engineers in each field. However, as technology advances and continues to expand its presence into all areas of society the need for technicians and technologists to develop, run, and maintain this technology will also grow. The Bureau of Labor Statistics states that the overall employment of technicians and technologists is expected to expand as fast as the average for all occupations through 2010. As a result of the September 11, 2001, terrorist attacks on the United States, it is likely that the new efforts at security both at home and abroad will rely heavily on expanded and new uses of technology, which is favorable to the job outlook for technicians and technologists.

EARNINGS

The earnings for engineering technicians and technologists vary widely with the occupational specialization. According to the Bureau of Labor Statistics the median annual earnings of electrical and electronics engineering technicians were $40,020 in 2000, with the middle 50 percent earning between $31,570 and $49,680. The average annual earnings for civil engineering, mechanical engineering, and aerospace engineering technicians were $35,990, $53,340, and $40,580 respectively for 2000. Other occupational specialties can expect similar earnings. The exception has been for industrial engineering technicians in computer and data processing. These technicians earned an average of $73,320 in 2000.

ADDITIONAL SOURCES OF INFORMATION

A list of accredited programs in all engineering fields is available from:

American Board of Engineering and Technology, Inc.
111 Market Place, Suite 1050
Baltimore, MD 21202
abet.org

A full package of guidance materials and information (product number SP-01) on a variety of engineering technician and technology careers can be purchased from the Junior Engineering Technical Society (JETS) at the following address. Free information is available on the JETS website.

Junior Engineering Technical Society (JETS)
1420 King Street, Suite 405
Alexandria, VA 22314-2794
jets.org

As a college student, you can join a number of social, honorary, and professional organizations affiliated with engineering technology. Once you are a practicing technologist, you can become certified in recognition of your capabilities. Practicing engineering technologists can join professional organizations such as the following:

American Society of Certified Engineering Technicians (ASCET)
2029 K Street NW
Washington, DC 20006
ascet.org

Additional information on certification of engineering technicians is available from the following organization:

National Institute for Certification in Engineering Technologies
   (NICET)
1420 King Street
Alexandria, VA 22314-2794
nicet.net

APPENDIX

A

U.S. UNIVERSITIES OFFERING ENGINEERING PROGRAMS

The following list of U.S. universities offering engineering programs was provided by the American Society for Engineering Education (2001). The Accreditation Board for Engineering and Technology (ABET) lists all ABET-accredited schools and programs at its website, abet.org/accredited_prgs.html.

American University (american.edu)

Appalachian State University (appstate.edu)

Arizona State University; College of Engineering and Applied Sciences (eas.asu.edu)

Auburn University; College of Engineering (eng.auburn.edu)

Ball State University (bsu.edu)

Baylor University (baylor.edu)

Binghamton University (binghamton.edu)

Bloomsburg University ((bloomu.edu)

Boise State University (idbsu.edu)

Boston University; College of Engineering (http://web.bu.edu/eng/)

Bradley University; College of Engineering and Technology (bradley.edu/academics/eng/eng.html)

Brigham Young University; College of Engineering and Technology (et.byu.edu)

Brown University (brown.edu)

Bucknell University; College of Engineering (eg.bucknell.edu)

California Institute of Technology; Division of Engineering and
    Applied Science (caltech.edu/caltech/EandAS.html)

California Polytechnic State University (calpoly.edu)

California State Polytechnic University; Pomona College of
    Engineering (csupomona.edu/~engineering)

California State University–Chico; College of Engineering, Computer
    Science, and Technology (ecst.csuchico.edu)

California State University–Fresno; School of Engineering
    (engr.csufresno.edu)

California State University–Fullerton; School of Engineering and
    Computer Science (ecs.fullerton.edu)

California State University–Hayward (csuhayward.edu)

California State University–Long Beach; College of Engineering
    (engr.csulb.edu)

California State University–Northridge (csun.edu)

California State University–Sacramento; School of Engineering and
    Computer Science (csus.edu)

California State University–San Marcos (csusm.edu)

California State University–Stanislaus (http://lead.csustan.edu)

Catholic University of America; School of Engineering (ee.cua.edu)

Carnegie Mellon University; Carnegie Institute of Technology
    (cit.cmu.edu)

Case Western Reserve University; Case School of Engineering
    (case.cwru.edu)

Central Washington University (cwu.edu)

Christian Brothers University; School of Engineering (cbu.edu)

Christopher Newport University (pcs.cnu.edu)

The Citadel; Department of Civil Engineering (http://cee.citadel.edu)

City University of New York (cuny.edu)

Clarkson University (clarkson.edu)

Clemson University; College of Engineering
    (http://gn.mines.colorado.edu/Academic/eng)

Cleveland State University (csuohio.edu)

Colorado School of Mines; Division of Engineering
    (eng.mines.colorado.edu:3862/1)

Colorado State University (colostate.edu)

Columbia University; School of Engineering and Applied Science (seas.columbia.edu/columbia)

Cooper Union for the Advancement of Science and Art; Albert Nerken School of Engineering (cooper.edu/engineering/Welcome.html)

Creighton University (cobweb.creighton.edu)

Cornell University; College of Engineering (engr.cornell.edu)

Dakota State University (dsu.edu)

Dartmouth College; Thayer School of Engineering (http://engineering.dartmouth.edu/thayer)

Denison University (denison.edu)

DePaul University (depaul.edu)

Drake University (drake.edu/index.html)

Drexel University; College of Engineering (coe.drexel.edu/coe.home/CoE.Home.html)

Duke University; School of Engineering (egr.duke.edu)

Duquesne University (duq.edu)

East Stroudsburg State University (esu.edu)

East Tennessee State University (etsu-tn.edu)

Embry-Riddle Aeronautical University (http://macwww.db.erau.edu)

Emory University (emory.edu)

Fisk University (fisk.edu)

Florida Institute of Technology (fit.edu)

Florida International University; College of Engineering and Design (eng.fiu.edu)

Florida State University; College of Engineering (eng.fsu.edu)

Furman University (furman.edu)

Gallaudet University (gallaudet.edu)

George Mason University; School of Information Technology and Engineering (ite.gmu.edu)

The George Washington University; School of Engineering and Applied Science (http://tangle.seas.gwu.edu/~seaswww)

Georgetown University (georgetown.edu)

Georgia Institute of Technology; College of Engineering (coe.gatech.edu)

Georgia State University (gsu.edu)

Hamline University (hamline.edu)

Harvard University (harvard.edu)

Harvey Mudd College (hmc.edu)

Hofstra University (hofstra.edu)

Howard University; School of Engineering
(cldc.howard.edu/HU/Schools/Engineering)

Humboldt State University (http://sorrel.humboldt.edu)

Idaho State University (isu.edu)

Illinois Institute of Technology; Department of Electrical and
Computer Engineering (ede.iit.edu)

Illinois State University (ilstu.edu)

Indiana Institute of Technology (indtech.edu)

Indiana University (indiana.edu)

Indiana University of Pennsylvania (iup.edu)

Indiana University Purdue University–Indianapolis; Purdue School of
Engineering and Technology (engr.iupui.edu)

Iowa State University; College of Engineering (eng.iastate.edu)

Jacksonville State University (http://jsucc.edu/home.html)

Johns Hopkins University; Whiting School of Engineering
(jhu.edu/~wse1/indexf.html)

Kansas State University; College of Engineering (engg.ksu.edu)

Kent State University (kent.edu)

Kettering University (kettering.edu)

Lehigh University; College of Engineering and Applied Science
(lehigh.edu/~ineas/eng/engineering.html)

Louisiana State University (lsu.edu)

Louisiana Tech University (latech.edu)

Loyola University–Chicago (luc.edu)

Manhattan College; School of Engineering
(manhattan.edu/engineer/engrpage.html)

Mankato State University (mankato.msus.edu)

Mansfield University (mnsfld.edu)

Marquette University; College of Engineering (eng.mu.edu)

Marshall University; College of Science (marshall.edu/cos)

Massachusetts Institute of Technology; School of Engineering
(http://web.mit.edu/org/e/engineering/www)

Miami University of Ohio; School of Applied Science
(sas.muohio.edu)

Michigan State University; College of Engineering
(http://web.egr.msu.edu)

Michigan Technological University (mtu.edu)

Milwaukee School of Engineering (msoe.edu)

Mississippi State University (msstate.edu)

Monmouth University (monmouth.edu)

Montana State University–Bozeman (montana.edu)

National Technological University (ntu.edu)

New Jersey Institute of Technology (njit.edu)

New Mexico Tech (nmt.edu)

New Mexico State University; College of Engineering
(nmsu.edu/~coe)

New York University (nyu.edu)

Nicholls State University (http://server.nich.edu)

North Carolina State University; College of Engineering
(engr.ncsu.edu)

Northeastern University; College of Engineering (coe.neu.edu)

Northern Michigan University (nmu.edu)

Northwestern State University (nsula.edu)

Northwestern University (mccormick.northwestern.edu)

Nova Southeastern University (nova.edu)

Oakland University; School of Engineering and Applied Science
(secs.oakland.edu)

Ohio Northern University; T. J. Smull College of Engineering
(onu.edu/Engineering)

Ohio State University; College of Engineering (eng.ohio-state.edu)

Ohio University; Russ College of Engineering (ent.ohiou.edu)

Oklahoma Christian University of Science and Arts; College of
Science and Engineering (oc.edu/colleges/sci&eng/iens/
home.htm)

Oklahoma State University (http://osu.okstate.edu)

Old Dominion University; College of Engineering and Technology
(eng.odu.edu)

Oregon Graduate Institute of Science and Technology (ogi.edu)

Oregon State University; College of Engineering (engr.orst.edu)

Pennsylvania State University; College of Engineering (engr.psu.edu)

Polytechnic University (poly.edu)

Portland State University; School of Engineering and Applied Science (eas.pdx.edu)

Prairie View A&M University (pvamu.edu)

Princeton University; School of Engineering and Applied Science (princeton.edu/~seasweb)

Purdue University; School of Engineering (ecn.purdue.edu)

Rensselaer Polytechnic Institute; School of Engineering (eng.rpi.edu)

Rice University (rice.edu)

Rochester Institute of Technology; College of Engineering (rit.edu/~630www)

Rockefeller University (rockefeller.edu)

Rowan University; School of Engineering (sun00.rowan.edu/index.html)

Rutgers University (rutgers.edu)

Sam Houston State University (shsu.edu)

San Diego State University; College of Engineering (http://kahuna.sdsu.edu.engineering)

Santa Clara University; School of Engineering (engr.scu.edu)

Seton Hall University (shu.edu)

Sonoma State University (sonoma.edu)

South Dakota School of Mines and Technology (sdsmt.edu)

Southwest Texas State University (swt.edu)

Stanford University; School of Engineering (http://soe.stanford.edu/soe.html)

State University of New York (suny.edu)

State University of New York–Buffalo; School of Engineering and Applied Sciences (eng.buffalo.edu)

Stevens Institute of Technology (stevens-tech.edu)

Syracuse University; School of Engineering and Computer Science (ecs.syr.edu)

Temple University (temple.edu)

Texas A&M University (tamu.edu)

Texas A&M University–Kingsville; College of Engineering (engineer.tamuk.edu)

Texas Christian University; Department of Engineering (engr.tcu.edu)

Texas Tech University; College of Engineering (coe.ttu.edu)

Thomas Jefferson University (tju.edu)

Trinity University; Engineering Science (engr.trinity.edu)

Tufts University (tufts.edu)

Tulane University (tulane.edu)

Union College (union.edu)

United States Air Force Academy (usafa.af.mil)

United States Military Academy (usma.edu)

University of Alabama–Huntsville; College of Engineering (http://info.uah.edu/engdata.html)

University of Alaska (alaska.edu)

University of Arizona; College of Engineering and Mines (engr.arizona.edu)

University of Arkansas–Fayetteville; College of Engineering (http://web.engr.uark.edu)

University of Arkansas–Little Rock (ualr.edu)

University of Arkansas–Monticello (uamont.edu)

University of California–Berkeley; College of Engineering (coe.berkeley.edu)

University of California–Davis (ucdavis.edu)

University of California–Irvine; School of Engineering (eng.uci.edu)

University of California–Los Angeles; School of Engineering and Applied Science (seas.ucla.edu)

University of California–Riverside; Marlan and Rosemary Bourns College of Engineering (http://engr.ucr.edu)

University of California–San Diego; School of Engineering (http://www-soe.ucsd.edu)

University of California–San Francisco (ucsf.edu)

University of California–Santa Barbara; College of Engineering (ece.ucsb.edu)

University of California–Santa Cruz; Division of Engineering (cse.ucsc.edu)

University of Central Arkansas (uca.edu)

University of Central Florida (ucf.edu)

University of Chicago (uchicago.edu)

University of Cincinnati; College of Engineering (eng.uc.edu)

University of Colorado–Boulder; College of Engineering and Applied Science (colorado.edu/engineering)

University of Connecticut; School of Engineering (eng2.uconn.edu)

University of Dayton; School of Engineering (engr.udayton.edu)

University of Delaware; College of Engineering (udel.edu/engg)

University of Florida; College of Engineering (eng.ufl.edu)

University of Georgia (uga.edu)

University of Hartford; College of Engineering (http://uhavax.hartford.edu/~engineer/engineer.html)

University of Hawaii System; University of Hawaii at Manoa College of Engineering (eng.hawaii.edu)

University of Houston; Cullen College of Engineering (ngr.uh.edu)

University of Idaho (uidaho.edu/uidaho-home.html)

University of Illinois–Chicago (uic.edu)

University of Illinois–Urbana-Champaign; College of Engineering (engr.uiuc.edu)

University of Iowa; College of Engineering (icaen.uiowa.edu)

University of Kansas (ukans.edu)

University of Kentucky–Lexington; College of Engineering (engr.uky.edu)

University of Louisville; J. B. Speed Scientific School (spd.louisville.edu)

University of Maine (maine.edu)

University of Maryland–Baltimore County (umbc.edu)

University of Maryland–College Park; A. J. Clark School of Engineering and Glenn L. Martin Institute of Technology (engr.umd.edu/maryland.htm)

University of Massachusetts System (umassp.edu)

University of Massachusetts–Amherst; College of Engineering (ecs.umass.edu)

University of Massachusetts–Dartmouth; College of Engineering (ece.umassd.edu)

University of Massachusetts–Lowell; College of Engineering (eng.uml.edu/~jbfranc)

University of Memphis (memphis.edu)

University of Miami; College of Engineering (eng.miami.edu)

University of Michigan–Ann Arbor (umich.edu)

University of Michigan–Dearborn; School of Engineering (engin.umd.umich.edu)

University of Minnesota (umn.edu)

University of Minnesota–Duluth; College of Science and Engineering (d.umn.edu/cse)

University of Mississippi (olemiss.edu)

University of Missouri–Columbia; College of Engineering (ecn.missouri.edu)

University of Missouri–Kansas City (umkc.edu)

University of Missouri–Rolla; School of Engineering (eng.umr.edu)

University of Nebraska–Lincoln (unl.edu/index.html)

University of Nebraska–Omaha; College of Engineering and Technology (cet-omaha.unomaha.edu)

University of Nevada–Las Vegas; Howard R. Hughes College of Engineering (egr.unlv.edu)

University of Nevada–Reno (unr.edu)

University of New Hampshire (unh.edu)

University of New Haven (newhaven.edu)

University of New Mexico; School of Engineering (cs.unm.edu/soe)

University of North Carolina–Asheville (unca.edu)

University of North Carolina–Chapel Hill; Department of Environmental Sciences and Engineering (sph.unc.edu/envr)

University of North Carolina–Charlotte; William States Lee College of Engineering (coe.uncc.edu)

University of North Florida (unf.edu)

University of North Texas (unt.edu)

University of Northern Iowa (uni.edu)

University of Notre Dame; Department of Computer Science and Engineering (cse.nd.edu)

University of Oklahoma (ou.edu)

University of Oregon (uoregon.edu)

University of the Pacific; School of Engineering (cs.uop.edu/eng/school_of_engineering.html)

University of Pennsylvania; School of Engineering and Applied Science (seas.upenn.edu)

University of Pittsburgh; School of Engineering (engrng.pitt.edu)

University of Portland; Multnomah School of Engineering (up.edu/academics/engineering/default.html)

University of Rhode Island; College of Engineering (egr.uri.edu)

University of Rochester; School of Engineering and Applied Sciences (ceas.rochester.edu:8080)

University of San Francisco (usfca.edu)

University of South Alabama; College of Engineering (eng.usouthal.edu)

University of Southern California; School of Engineering (usc.edu/dept/engineering/EngSchool.html)

University of South Carolina; College of Engineering (engr.sc.edu)

University of South Florida; College of Engineering (eng.usf.edu)

University of Southern Maine; School of Applied Science (ee.usm.maine.edu/sas)

University of Southern Mississippi (usm.edu)

University of Southwestern Louisiana (usl.edu)

University of Tennessee–Chattanooga; College of Engineering (utc.edu/~engrcs/index.html)

University of Tennessee–Knoxville; College of Engineering (engr.utk.edu)

University of Tennessee Space Institute (utsi.edu)

University of Texas–Arlington (uta.edu)

University of Texas–Austin (utexas.edu)

University of Texas–Dallas; Erik Jonsson School of Engineering and Computer Science (utdallas.edu/dept/eecs)

University of Texas–San Antonio; College of Sciences and Engineering (http://voyager1.utsa.edu)

University of Toledo; College of Engineering (eng.utoledo.edu)

University of Utah (utah.edu)

University of Vermont; Division of Engineering, Mathematics and Business Administration (emba.uvm.edu)

University of Virginia; School of Engineering and Applied Science (seas.virginia.edu)

University of Washington; College of Engineering (engr.washington.edu)

University of Wisconsin–Madison; College of Engineering (engr.wisc.edu)

University of Wisconsin–Milwaukee; College of Engineering and Applied Science (cae.uwm.edu)

University of Wisconsin–Oshkosh (uwosh.edu)

University of Wyoming; College of Engineering (eng.uwyo.edu)

Utah State University (usu.edu)

Vanderbilt University (vanderbilt.edu/Default.html)

Virginia Commonwealth University (egr.vcu.edu)

Virginia Military Institute (vmi.edu)

Virginia Tech; College of Engineering (eng.vt.edu)

Wake Forest University (wfu.edu/indexv.html)

Washington and Lee University (wlu.edu)

Washington State University (wsu.edu)

Washington University–St. Louis; School of Engineering and Applied Science (seas.wustl.edu)

Wesleyan University (wesleyan.edu)

West Virginia University; College of Engineering (coe.wvu.edu)

Western Kentucky University (wku.edu)

Western Washington University (wwu.edu)

Wichita State University; College of Engineering (engr.twsu.edu)

Wilkes University (wilkes.edu)

Willamette University (willamette.edu)

Worcester Polytechnic Institute (wpi.edu)

Wright State University; College of Engineering and Computer Science (cs.wright.edu)

Yale University; Faculty of Engineering (eng.yale.edu)

Youngstown State University (ysu.edu)

A P P E N D I X

B

SCHOLARSHIPS

The following organizations offer information on engineering scholarships, minority engineering scholarships, or other miscellaneous scholarships that may apply to engineering students. At the end of this appendix is a list of free online scholarship search services.

ENGINEERING SCHOLARSHIPS

American Nuclear Society
ans.org/pi/students/scholarships

American Society of Agricultural Engineers
asae.org/membership/studentmanual.html

American Society of Mechanical Engineers
asme.org/education/enged/aid/index.htm

The Institute of Electrical and Electronic Engineers
ieee.org/membership/students/sc_scholarships.html

The American Ceramic Society
acers.org/membership/levels/studentopportunities.asp

National Association of Professional Engineers
nspe.org/aboutnspe/ab1-scholarships.asp

American Institute of Aeronautics and Astronautics
aiaa.org/education/index.hfm?edu=0

American Chemical Society
http://chemistry.org/portal/Chemistry?PID=acsdisplay.html&DOC=
    minorityaffairs%5Cscholars.html

SAE Engineering Scholarships
sae.org/students/engschlr.htm

American Geological Institute
agiweb.org/education/mpp.html

American Institute of Physics
aip.org/education/sps

American Welding Society Foundation
aws.org/foundation

American Society for Metals
asminternational.org//content/Foundation/UndergraduateScholarships/
    Undergraduate.htm

American Congress of Surveying and Mapping (ACSM)
6 Montgomery Village Avenue, Suite 403
Gaithersburg, MD 20879
acsm.net/scholar.html

American Council of Independent Laboratories (ACIL)
1629 K Street NW, Suite 400
Washington, DC 20006
acil.org/about/scholarship.html

American Concrete Institute (ACI)
P.O. Box 9094
Farmington Hills, MI 48333
aci-int.org

American Society of Body Engineers (ASBE)
2122 Fifteen Mile Road, Suite F
Sterling Heights, MI 48310
asbe.net/scholarship.htm

American Society for Nondestructive Testing (ASNT)
1711 Arlingate Lane
P.O. Box 28518
Columbus, OH 43228-0518
asnt.org/keydocuments/awards/awards.htm

American Society of Heating, Refrigerating and Air-Conditioning
    Engineers (ASHRAE)
1791 Tullie Circle NE
Atlanta, GA 30329
ashrae.org

American Society of Naval Engineers (ASNE)
1452 Duke Street
Alexandria, VA 22314
navalengineers.org/scholarships/sc_info.htm

American Society of Plumbing Engineers (ASPE)
3617 Thousand Oaks Boulevard, Suite 210
Westlake Village, CA 91362-3649
aspe.org/ASPE_Scholarship98/Steele_Scholarship.html

American Society of Safety Engineers (ASSE)
1800 East Oakton Street
Des Plaines, IL 60018
asse.org

Association for Engineering Geologists
Department of Geology and Geophysics
Texas A&M University
TAMU 3115
College Station, TX 77843-3115
aegweb.org/foundation/index.html

Institute of Industrial Engineers (IIE)
25 Technology Park
Norcross, GA 30092
http://128.241.229.4/public/articles/index.cfm?Cat=226

Instrumentation, Systems and Automation Society (ISA)
P.O. Box 12277
67 Alexander Drive
Research Triangle Park, NC 27709
isa.org/educationfoundation/1,3090,0,00.html

International Association of Lighting Designers (IALD)
The Merchandise Mart
200 World Trade Center, Suite 487
Chicago, IL 60654
iald.org

Nuclear Energy Institute (NEI)
1776 I Street NW, Suite 400
Washington, DC 20006
nei.org/index.asp?catnum=2&catid=210

Society for Mining, Metallurgy, and Exploration
8307 Shaffer Parkway
Littleton, CO 80127-4102
smenet.org/education/students/sme_scholarships.cfm?CFID=
    879540&CFTOKEN=45154546

Society of Manufacturing Engineers (SME)
One SME Drive
P.O. Box 930
Dearborn, MI 48121-0930
sme.org/cgi-bin/smeefhtml.pl?/foundation/scholarships/
    fsfstudp.htm&&&SME&

Society of Naval Architects and Marine Engineers
601 Pavonia Avenue
Jersey City, NJ 07306
sname.org/membership/Scholar.html

Society of Petroleum Engineers
P.O. Box 833836
Richardson, TX 75083-3836
spe.org/spe/cda/views/shared/viewChannelsMaster/0,2883,1648_2388_
    5329_4996,00.html#SPETop

Society of Plastics Engineers (SPE)
14 Fairfield Drive
Brookfield, CT 06804-0403
4spe.org/grantsscholarships/scholarships.htm

SPIE—International Society for Optical Engineering
P.O. Box 10
Bellingham, WA 98227-0010
spie.org/CommunityServices/StudentsAndEducators/index.cfm?fuse
    action=Scholarships

Technical Association of the Pulp and Paper Industry (TAPPI)
P.O. Box 105113
Norcross, GA 30092
tappi.org/index.asp?ip=-1&ch=16&rc=-1

The Minerals, Metals, and Materials Society (TMS)
184 Thorn Hill Road
Warrendale, PA 15086-7514
tms.org/Students/AwardsPrograms/Scholarships.html

Families of Freedom Scholarship Fund (for especially needy dependents
of victims of the September 11, 2001, attacks)
aps.org/sciencefund.html

WOMEN AND MINORITIES IN ENGINEERING SCHOLARSHIPS

Diversity Engineering Scholarship Program (University of Tennessee
program aimed at African-Americans—allied with the cooperative
engineering program)
engr.utk.edu/desp

Marty E. Blaylock Engineering Scholarship (established by Monsanto for
underrepresented engineering students)
black-collegian.com/news/blaylock501.shtml

The Guide to Graduate and Professional School Fellowships
imdiversity.com/employerprofiles/grad_school/gs_fellowcontents.asp

National Society of Black Engineers (NSBE)
nsbe.org/scholarships/index.html

American Indian Science and Engineering Society
aises.org/scholarships/index.html

Society of Hispanic Engineers
shpefoundation.org/scholarship-program.html

Society of Women Engineers
swe.org/SWE/StudentServices/Scholarship/brochure.htm

MISCELLANEOUS SCHOLARSHIPS

Scholarship News (non–engineering specific—includes minority and
  engineering scholarship links)
free-4u.com/minority.htm

FREE ONLINE SCHOLARSHIP SEARCH SERVICES

FastWeb
fastweb.com

CollegeNET
collegenet.com

College Board Online
collegeboard.org

ScienceWise.com
http://content.sciencewise.com

GoCollege
gocollege.com

SRN Express
srnexpress.com

Absolutely Scholarships
scholaraid.com

WiredScholar
wiredscholar.com

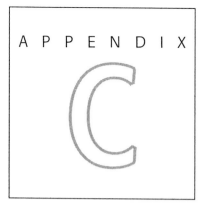

APPENDIX C

GENERAL ENGINEERING SOCIETIES

Accrediting Board of Engineering and Technology (ABET)
111 Market Place, Suite 1050
Baltimore, MD 21202-4012
abet.org

American Association of Engineering Societies, Inc. (AAES)
1111 Nineteenth Street NW, Suite 403
Washington, DC 20036
asee.org/aaes

American Consulting Engineers Council (ACEC)
1015 Fifteenth Street NW, Suite 802
Washington, DC 20005
acec.org

American Council of Engineering Companies
1015 Fifteenth Street NW
Washington, DC 20005
acec.org
Coalitions and special interest groups:
Council of American Structural Engineers (CASE)
Council of Professional Surveyors (COPS)
Design Professionals Coalition (DPC)

Environmental Business Action Coalition (EBAC)

Research Management Foundation (RMF)

Small Firm Council (SFC)

American Society for Engineering Education (ASEE)
1818 N Street NW, Suite 600
Washington, DC 20036
asee.org

Junior Engineering Technical Society
1420 King Street, Suite 405
Alexandria, VA 22314
jets.org

National Academy of Engineering
2101 Constitution Avenue NW
Washington, DC 20418
nae.edu

National Academy of Sciences
2101 Constitution Avenue NW
Washington, DC 20418
nas.edu

National Action Council for Minorities in Engineering, Inc. (NACME)
The Empire State Building
350 Fifth Avenue, Suite 2212
New York, NY 10118-2299
nacme.org

National Society of Professional Engineers (NSPE)
1420 King Street
Alexandria, VA 22314
nspe.org

Society of Women Engineers
120 Wall Street, Eleventh Floor
New York, NY 10005-3902
swe.org

APPENDIX

ABET MEMBER SOCIETIES AND DISCIPLINES

American Academy of Environmental Engineers (AAEE)
130 Holiday Court, Suite 100
Annapolis, MD 21404
aaee.net
Environmental engineering
Environmental engineering technology

American Congress on Surveying and Mapping (ACSM)
6 Montgomery Village Avenue, Suite 403
Gaithersburg, MD 20879
acsm.net
Surveying
Surveying engineering
Survey engineering technology

American Industrial Hygiene Association (AIHA)
2700 Prosperity Avenue, Suite 250
Fairfax, VA 22031
aiha.org
Industrial hygiene

American Institute of Aeronautics and Astronautics (AIAA)
1801 Alexander Bell Drive
Reston, VA 20191-4344
aiaa.org
Aerospace engineering
Aerospace engineering technology

American Institute of Chemical Engineers (AIChE)
Three Park Avenue
New York, NY 10016-5901
aiche.org
Chemical engineering
Chemical engineering technology

American Nuclear Society (ANS)
555 North Kensington Avenue
La Grange Park, IL 60525
ans.org
Nuclear engineering
Nuclear engineering technology

American Society of Agricultural Engineers (ASAE)
2950 Niles Road
St. Joseph, MI 49085
http://asae.org
Agricultural engineering
Biological engineering
Agricultural engineering technology
Forest engineering

American Society of Civil Engineers
1801 Alexander Bell Drive
Reston, VA 20191-4400
asce.org
Architectural engineering
Architectural engineering technology
Civil engineering

Civil engineering technology
Construction engineering
Construction engineering technology

American Society for Engineering Education (ASEE)
1818 N Street NW, Suite 600
Washington, DC 20036
asee.org

American Society of Heating, Refrigerating and Air-Conditioning
 Engineers (ASHRAE)
1791 Tullie Circle NE
Atlanta, GA 30329
ashrae.org
Air-conditioning engineering
Air-conditioning engineering technology

American Society of Mechanical Engineers (ASME)
Three Park Avenue
New York, NY 10016-5990
asme.org
Mechanical engineering
Mechanical engineering technology
Drafting/design engineering technology (mechanical)
Engineering mechanics

Computing Sciences Accreditation Board, Inc.
184 North Street
Stamford, CT 06901
csab.org
Computer science
Software engineering

Institute of Electrical and Electronics Engineers
IEEE Service Center
445 Hoes Lane
P.O. Box 1331
Piscataway, NJ 08855-1331

ieee.org
Bioengineering
Bioengineering technology
Computer engineering
Computer engineering technology
Electromechanical engineering technology
Electrical and electronics engineering
Electrical and electronics engineering technology
Telecommunications engineering technology

Institute of Industrial Engineers
25 Technology Park/Atlanta
Norcross, GA 30092
iienet.org
Industrial engineering
Industrial engineering technology
Engineering management

The International Society for Measurement and Control (ISA)
67 Alexander Drive
P.O. Box 12277
Research Triangle Park, NC 27709
isa.org
Instrumentation engineering technology

National Council of Examiners for Engineering and Surveying (NCEES)
P.O. Box 1686
Clemson, SC 29633-1686
ncees.org

National Institute of Ceramic Engineers (NICE)
c/o Diane Folz, Executive Director
NICE
Department of Materials Science Engineering
P.O. Box 116400
Gainesville, FL 32611-6400
ceramics.org

Ceramic engineering
Ceramic engineering technology

National Society of Professional Engineers (NSPE)
1420 King Street
Alexandria, VA 22314
nspe.org

Society of Automotive Engineers (SAE)
400 Commonwealth Drive
Warrendale, PA 15096
sae.org
Automotive engineering
Automotive engineering technology

Society of Manufacturing Engineers
One SME Drive
P.O. Box 930
Dearborn, MI 48121
sme.org
Manufacturing engineering
Manufacturing engineering technology

Society for Mining, Metallurgy and Exploration, Inc. (SME-AIME)
8307 Shaffer Parkway
P.O. Box 625002
Littleton, CO 80162-5002
smenet.org
Geological/geophysical engineering
Mining engineering
Mining engineering technology
Mineral engineering

Society of Naval Architects and Marine Engineers (SNAME)
601 Pavonia Avenue
Jersey City, NJ 07306
sname.org

Ocean engineering
Naval architecture and marine engineering
Marine engineering technology

Society of Petroleum Engineers
P.O. Box 833836
Richardson, TX 75083-3836
spe.org
Petroleum engineering
Petroleum engineering technology

The Minerals, Metals and Materials Society (TMS)
184 Thorn Hill Road
Warrendale, PA 15086
tms.org
Welding engineering
Welding engineering technology
Materials engineering
Metallurgical engineering
Metallurgical engineering technology

AFFILIATE SOCIETY MEMBERS

American Council of Engineering Companies
1015 Fifteenth Street NW
Washington, DC 20005
acec.org

American Institute of Mining, Metallurgical and Petroleum Engineers
   (AIME)
345 East Forty-Seventh Street
New York, NY 10017-2397
http://aimeny.org

American Society of Safety Engineers
1800 East Oakton Street
Des Plaines, IL 60018-2187
asse.org

Materials Research Society (MRS)
9800 McKnight Road
Pittsburgh, PA 15237
mrs.org

Society of Plastics Engineers (SPE)
14 Fairfield Drive
Brookfield Center, CT 06805
4spe.org

COGNIZANT TECHNICAL SOCIETY MEMBERS

American Society for Quality (ASQ)
611 East Wisconsin Avenue
P.O. Box 3005
Milwaukee, WI 53201-3005
asq.org

Health Physics Society (HPS)
1313 Dolly Madison Boulevard, Suite 402
McLean, VA 22101
hps.org

ABOUT THE AUTHOR

Dr. Geraldine Garner is the president of Science and Technology Career Strategies, Inc. Previously Garner was associate dean and associate professor of the Walter P. Murphy Cooperative Engineering Education Program at Northwestern University and taught graduate and undergraduate courses in career development at Northwestern University and Virginia Commonwealth University. She is the author of numerous engineering career books and articles.